Kubernetes for Absolute Beginners

Getting Familiar with K8s and Container Technologies

Brando Marzio Sabatini

Apress®

Kubernetes for Absolute Beginners: Getting Familiar with K8s and Container Technologies

Brando Marzio Sabatini
Computing Infrastructure Engineer,
CERN – European Organization for Nuclear Research,
Meyrin, Switzerland

ISBN-13 (pbk): 979-8-8688-2444-9 ISBN-13 (electronic): 979-8-8688-2445-6
https://doi.org/10.1007/979-8-8688-2445-6

Managing Director, Apress Media LLC: Welmoed Spahr
Acquisitions Editor: James Robinson-Prior
Editorial Assistant: Gryffin Winkler

Cover designed by eStudioCalamar

Distributed to the book trade worldwide by Springer Science+Business Media New York, 1 New York Plaza, New York, NY 10004. Phone 1-800-SPRINGER, fax (201) 348-4505, e-mail orders-ny@springer-sbm.com, or visit www.springeronline.com. Apress Media, LLC is a Delaware LLC and the sole member (owner) is Springer Science + Business Media Finance Inc (SSBM Finance Inc). SSBM Finance Inc is a Delaware corporation.

For information on translations, please e-mail booktranslations@springernature.com; for reprint, paperback, or audio rights, please e-mail bookpermissions@springernature.com.

Apress titles may be purchased in bulk for academic, corporate, or promotional use. eBook versions and licenses are also available for most titles. For more information, reference our Print and eBook Bulk Sales web page at http://www.apress.com/bulk-sales.

Any source code or other supplementary material referenced by the author in this book is available to readers on GitHub. For more detailed information, please visit https://www.apress.com/gp/services/source-code.

If disposing of this product, please recycle the paper

To my mother,
who has always had the patience to support me in every situation.
And to my partner, who gave me the space to work on this project;
her support was truly indispensable.
And to Ikbal,
my friend with whom I started working together. Through our
projects, everything began, and they led me to start writing this
technical book solo. Thank you, my friend.
I am deeply grateful to my partner, who gave me the space to work on
this project; her support was truly indispensable.

Table of Contents

About the Author

Brando Marzio Sabatini is a Computing Infrastructure Engineer and technical author driven by a passion for innovation, experimentation, and systematic improvement of complex systems. His fascination with technology began in childhood, fueling a lifelong curiosity and determination to master new devices and systems.

With over 10 years of experience in the IT industry, Brando began his professional career as an IT specialist at one of the world's leading French retailers in Italy. He then expanded his expertise in Germany, serving as a technical engineer at a company specializing in hybrid cloud solutions, data services, and data storage, and afterwards as a Data Centre Operator at EUMETSAT, an intergovernmental organization managing critical meteorological infrastructure. His international experience continued with a position as Senior Associate Technical Support in Southeast Asia's oil and gas industry.

Currently, Brando works at CERN as a Computing Infrastructure Engineer, serving on the system administration team within the Experimental Physics (EP) Department, supporting the CMS Experiment as part of the Trigger and Data Acquisition (TDAQ) group. In this role, he performs Linux system administration across control room consoles, data centre servers, and virtual machines connected to the CMS experiment network, and contributes to the strategic design and evolution of CMS's online computing infrastructure — including networks, online clusters, mass storage, virtual machines, and container orchestration platforms. His day-to-day work spans hardware infrastructure, server management, and the operation of the full observability stack (Prometheus, Grafana, Mimir, Loki), alongside Kubernetes and Docker orchestration on RHEL and AlmaLinux systems. He also collaborates closely with end-users ranging from physicists to operations teams to diagnose and resolve complex operational problems, and participates in on-call duty for urgent system administration interventions.

Brando is dedicated to continuous learning and problem-solving, with a deep passion for improving systems and resolving complex technical challenges — particularly through systematic troubleshooting. He thrives on diagnosing issues and implementing efficient solutions, always seeking to enhance his skills and advance the field. His areas of expertise include hardware infrastructure, Linux system administration (AlmaLinux/RHEL), container technologies (Docker, Kubernetes), monitoring and observability tooling, and large-scale deployment and troubleshooting, where his methodical approach excels.

He holds two degrees: a Bachelor of Science (First Class Honours) in Computing and Information Technologies from the University of Derby, and a Bachelor of Engineering in Information Technology from Metropolia University of Applied Sciences in Finland. As an active learner, Brando is constantly seeking to expand his expertise, currently specializing in observability and private cloud infrastructure.

As co-founder and author of the blog ithands-on (later Hands On Tech Tips, 2016–2024), he championed accessible infrastructure education and the democratization of technical knowledge for nearly a decade. He continues to write and work, specializing across IT infrastructure while advancing his expertise in cloud-native operations and observability engineering.

About the Technical Reviewer

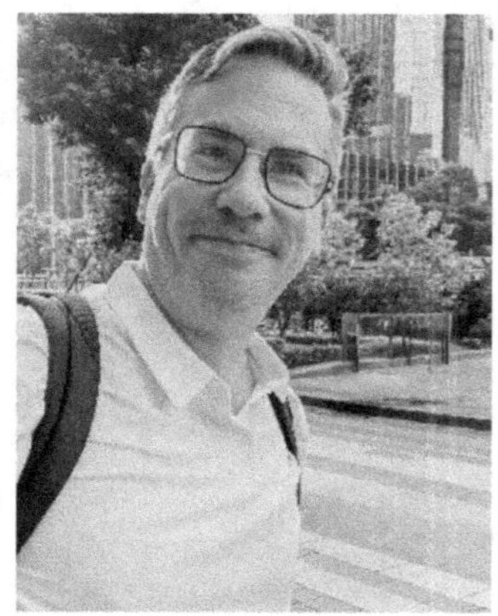 **Johannes Verwijnen** is a veteran developer and systems administrator who has been working with code and infrastructure since the 1990s. Today, he operates as a full-time authorized instructor for AWS, Google Cloud, Microsoft, and CompTIA. He also teaches Linux Foundation's Kubernetes Administration (LFS458) and Kubernetes for App Developers (LFD459). When not in the classroom, he tries his best to be a father.

Introduction

What Is This Book About?

Kubernetes has become the de facto standard for managing containerized applications at scale. Yet for those new to this technology, the abundance of commands, concepts, and configurations can feel overwhelming. This book takes a different approach: it assumes no prior Kubernetes knowledge and builds your understanding from the ground up, one concept at a time.

This book is a practical guide to Kubernetes fundamentals. Rather than presenting theoretical abstractions or jumping directly to production scenarios, we introduce core ideas through relatable analogies, walk through each concept systematically, and validate your understanding with hands-on examples. By the end, you'll have a working Kubernetes cluster running on your machine, the confidence to deploy applications to it, and a solid mental model of how Kubernetes operates.

Who Is This Book For?

This book is written for

- **System administrators** and **infrastructure operators** who manage on-premises or cloud environments and need to understand modern container orchestration

- **Software developers** curious about how their applications get packaged, deployed, and scaled in production

- **DevOps engineers** transitioning from traditional infrastructure management to cloud-native practices

- **Students and career changers** entering infrastructure technology without prior Kubernetes experience

- **IT professionals** who need to understand what Kubernetes is, why organizations adopt it, and how to work with it effectively

We assume you have basic familiarity with the Linux command line and virtual machines, but we don't assume any experience with containers, Docker, or orchestration platforms. If terms like "pod," "namespace," or "deployment" are unfamiliar, this book will clarify them all.

How This Book Is Structured

This book is organized into 20 chapters grouped into logical learning phases:

Part 1: Foundations (Chapters 1–5) establishes the context and core concepts. We begin by exploring what Kubernetes is, why it exists, and how it evolved from Google's internal infrastructure tools. We introduce Docker as the containerization platform that makes Kubernetes meaningful. We then examine the fundamental building blocks—clusters, nodes, and Pods—and walk through the architecture that makes Kubernetes orchestration possible.

Part 2: Working with Applications (Chapters 6–11) focuses on how you deploy and manage actual workloads. You'll learn to write Kubernetes manifests using YAML, manage containerized applications through Deployments and ReplicaSets, configure networking so your applications can communicate, and use ConfigMaps and Secrets to manage application configuration and sensitive data. You'll also explore how Kubernetes identifies and selects Pods using labels, selectors, and annotations.

Part 3: Organization and Operations (Chapters 12–18) addresses the operational concerns that matter in shared, multi-tenant environments. We examine Namespaces for logical isolation, health checks and liveness probes for application resilience, and how to distinguish between stateful and stateless workloads. We then move into advanced topics: storage solutions for persistent data, Jobs and DaemonSets for specialized workloads, and DNS service discovery that allows applications to find each other dynamically.

Part 4: Production Concerns (Chapters 19–20) covers the operational realities of running Kubernetes responsibly. We address resource management to prevent one application from starving others, examine certificates and encryption as the foundation of secure communication, and explore how Kubernetes protects data both in transit and at rest.

What You Will Learn

By reading this book, you will

- Understand what Kubernetes is, what problems it solves, and when it makes sense to use it

- Grasp the fundamental concepts: clusters, nodes, Pods, Deployments, and Services

- Write Kubernetes YAML manifests to define and deploy containerized applications

- Deploy applications to a working Kubernetes cluster and troubleshoot common issues

- Manage application configuration using ConfigMaps and Secrets

- Implement health checks and automated recovery for resilient applications

- Organize applications across namespaces and manage resource consumption fairly

- Understand how Kubernetes provides secure communication and protects sensitive data

- Know when and why to use different Kubernetes resources (Jobs, StatefulSets, DaemonSets, etc.)

- Recognize the limitations of your current knowledge and identify the next topics to explore

How to Use This Book

Read sequentially from Chapter 1. Each chapter builds on concepts introduced earlier. While it's tempting to skip directly to advanced topics, you'll find that skipping foundational chapters leads to confusion later.

Follow the hands-on examples. Some chapters include practical exercises using K3s, a lightweight Kubernetes distribution perfect for learning. Set up a virtual machine with Ubuntu, follow the installation instructions, and run the examples as you read. Understanding through doing is far more effective than reading alone.

Refer back often. Kubernetes involves many concepts that interact with one another. When you encounter something unclear, return to earlier chapters for context. A concept that seemed abstract in Chapter 3 will make perfect sense once you've deployed an actual application in a later chapter.

Take notes and experiment. After completing each chapter, try modifying the examples. Change the number of replicas, update configuration values, or deploy different container images. This experimentation builds intuition that pure reading cannot provide.

What You Won't Find Here

This book deliberately avoids certain advanced topics to maintain focus on fundamentals:

- **Production deployment strategies** beyond basic concepts (topics like GitOps, advanced CI/CD, and infrastructure-as-code practices are saved for later learning)

- **Cloud provider specifics** (we focus on core Kubernetes concepts that apply everywhere, though many cloud providers offer managed Kubernetes services that abstract away some complexity)

- **Advanced security configurations** (we cover the essentials of certificates and encryption; hardening production clusters requires additional expertise)

- **Performance tuning and optimization** (critical for large-scale deployments, but premature optimization distracts from learning fundamentals)

- **Kubernetes source code internals** (understanding how Kubernetes works is valuable; reading its code is a separate, advanced undertaking)

This book is a beginning, not an ending. After completing it, you'll be ready to dive into specialized topics like monitoring (Prometheus and Grafana), advanced networking (service mesh, ingress controllers), and specialized workload types that your specific use case demands.

The Learning Path Ahead

Your journey through this book follows a natural progression:

1. **Chapters** 1–3 answer the question: "What is Kubernetes and why does it matter?"

2. **Chapters** 4–5 address: "How is a Kubernetes cluster organized internally?"

3. **Chapters** 6–8 show you: "How do I define and deploy applications?"

4. **Chapters** 9–11 teach you: "How do applications find each other and access configuration?"

5. **Chapters** 12–17 explain: "How do I organize and manage workloads in practice?"

6. **Chapters** 18–20 cover: "What do I need to know about resources, security, and reliability?"

Each chapter builds on the previous one. There are no shortcuts through Kubernetes fundamentals.

A Final Word Before You Begin

Learning Kubernetes is achievable, but it requires patience. The platform reflects decades of experience managing large-scale infrastructure. Some concepts will click immediately; others will feel abstract until you see them in action. This is normal.

Throughout this book, we use analogies and familiar comparisons to make abstract concepts concrete. We introduce one idea at a time and show how ideas connect to the larger picture. We include hands-on exercises and diagrams so that reading translates into understanding.

The Kubernetes community is helpful and welcoming. If you get stuck, resources like the official documentation, community forums, and Slack channels are full of people ready to help. Learning in community makes the journey faster and more enjoyable.

Welcome to *Kubernetes for Absolute Beginners*. Let's begin.

CHAPTER 1

Introduction to Kubernetes and Containers

Introduction

Welcome to the Kubernetes universe. If we are picking up this book, we have likely heard the buzz surrounding "K8s" (the common abbreviation for Kubernetes) and how it has revolutionized the way we deploy software. However, before we dive into commands, clusters, and configurations, it is vital to understand the context: Where did this technology come from? Why do we need it? And what does it actually do?

In this opening chapter, we will build the foundation. We won't just look at definitions; we will look briefly at the story behind Kubernetes, how it compares to other tools we might have heard of, and the massive problems it solves with modern IT infrastructure. This context will make every subsequent chapter easier to understand.

Objectives

By the end of this chapter, we will be able to

- Define what Kubernetes and Containers are in simple terms

- Have a brief introduction to the history of Kubernetes from its origins at Google to the Cloud Native Computing Foundation (CNCF)

- Understand the landscape of container orchestration and how Kubernetes compares to alternatives like Docker Swarm and Apache Mesos

- Identify key use cases where Kubernetes excels in the real world

© Brando Marzio Sabatini 2026
B. M. Sabatini, *Kubernetes for Absolute Beginners*, https://doi.org/10.1007/979-8-8688-2445-6_1

What Is Kubernetes?

Kubernetes is a container orchestration system that we can use to automate the deployment, management, and scaling of containerized applications. For those of us who don't know, containerized apps are software packages that come with their code, dependencies, and configurations in lightweight, portable containers that can run consistently in an array of environments.

Therefore, it provides a robust framework to run distributed systems reliably, offering amazing features like load balancing, storage orchestration, and automated rollouts and rollbacks. However, at its core, Kubernetes helps developers and operators make things easier by managing complex software systems by organizing containers into logical units called pods, which can be easily deployed and scaled across a cluster of machines.

Brief introduction to the Kubernetes history: from Borg to K8s

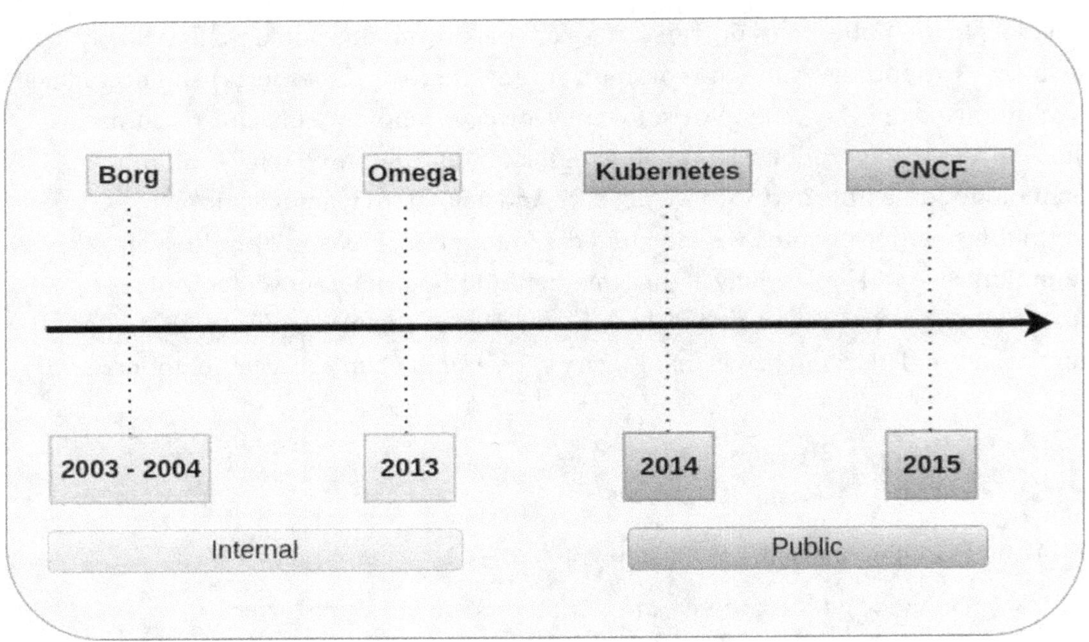

Figure 1-1. *Evolution of Kubernetes from internal tools to open source*

As we can imagine, Kubernetes did not appear out of nowhere. It has its roots in decades of experience managing infrastructure at one of the world's largest tech companies. Back in the early 2000s, Google faced a significant problem: they had thousands of applications running across massive data centers, and keeping track of them manually was impossible. To solve this, Google created a system called Borg around 2003. Borg was an internal tool designed to schedule and manage applications across clusters of machines. It handled the heavy lifting of deciding where applications should run, restarting them if they crashed, and making sure resources were used efficiently. While Borg worked well, Google knew it had limitations and room for improvement.

Around the same time, Google developed Omega, a parallel system that built upon Borg's concepts with improved shared state management and inter-system coordination. Though Omega had been in development internally since the late 2000s, it was first described publicly in a research paper in 2013. Omega took the lessons learned from Borg and built upon them with a more flexible architecture. It introduced new ideas about how to manage shared state across clusters and improved the way different systems could work together. Omega was Google's answer to making container management even more powerful and scalable. However, Google realized that keeping these tools internal was limiting their impact. The infrastructure challenges Google faced were the same ones many other companies were struggling with, and the industry needed a solution that everyone could use and improve together.

In 2014, Google decided to open-source their container orchestration knowledge and released Kubernetes to the world. The name itself means "helmsman" or "ship captain" in Greek, reflecting the idea of steering and managing containerized applications. Kubernetes drew heavily on Borg and Omega's proven concepts but was redesigned from the ground up with the open-source community in mind. This meant that developers everywhere could now access the same powerful orchestration tool that powered Google's infrastructure. The release marked a turning point in how organizations manage containers and applications at scale.

In 2015, Kubernetes v1.0 was released as the first production-ready version, and Google handed over the project to the Cloud Native Computing Foundation (CNCF), a neutral home for container orchestration. This move showed that Kubernetes was meant to be a community standard, not just a Google tool. Today, Kubernetes continues to evolve through contributions from thousands of developers and organizations around the world. The journey from Borg to Kubernetes shows how real-world problems at scale drive innovation and how opening up that innovation to the community creates something even more powerful (Figure 1-1).

What Are Containers?

Containers are executable units of software that are lightweight and that package an application's code along with all its dependencies, like binaries, libraries, configuration files, and runtime, in a single isolated environment. All this makes sure that the application can consistently run across various computing environments, whether on a developer's laptop, a testing server, or a production environment hosted in the cloud.

Within the topic of containers, it is important to mention the concept of "containerization," which basically refers to the process of packaging application code along with its dependencies into a portable container image. This process makes sure that applications can run seamlessly across various settings, removing the issues related to differences in configurations and dependencies between development, testing, and production environments.

Why Do We Have to Choose Kubernetes Today?

Because it simplifies the process of operating and expanding containerized workloads and increases efficiency, Kubernetes is still widely used and an excellent choice for managing modern applications. One of its main advantages is that it can ensure that applications are always accessible by automatically restarting failing containers and managing updates without downtime. It can also handle traffic distribution, storage management, and dynamic resource scaling based on demand. In terms of security, it has improved with features like stricter access control and automated vulnerability checks. By optimizing resource allocation, Kubernetes can help reduce infrastructure energy consumption, though this depends on how the underlying cluster is configured and managed. And its interoperability across cloud, on-premises, and multicloud environments makes it a reliable solution for any type of business.

Beyond these benefits, it is also essential to understand how Kubernetes differs from other container management systems such as Docker Swarm, Apache Mesos, or HashiCorp Nomad. Kubernetes is designed as a full-featured, extensible orchestration platform, offering rich built-in capabilities for service discovery, self-healing, horizontal and vertical auto-scaling, declarative configuration, and powerful networking primitives. While tools like Docker Swarm focus on simplicity and are well-suited for smaller or less complex clusters, they generally provide fewer advanced scheduling, policy, and extensibility features. Mesos, on the other hand, was built as a general-purpose cluster manager for many types of workloads (not just containers), which can make it more complex to adopt for typical cloud-native applications. Kubernetes has become the de facto standard because it strikes a balance between flexibility and standardization, backed by a massive ecosystem of tools, cloud-provider support, and an active open-source community, making it a future-proof choice for most organizations.

What Are the Use Cases Where We Could Use Kubernetes?

As there are multiple use cases for Kubernetes, for the scope of this book, we have selected the six use cases illustrated in Figure 1-2.

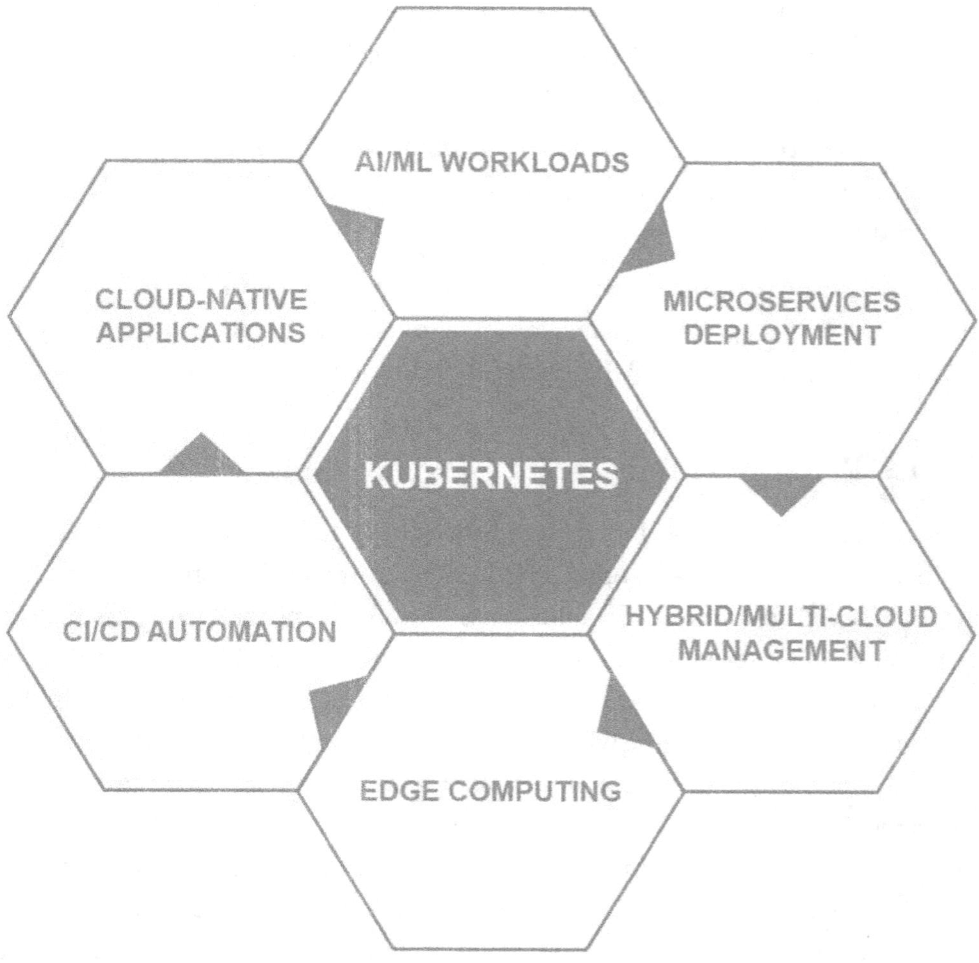

Figure 1-2. *Six core use cases of Kubernetes*

AI/ML workloads: Kubernetes is widely used to manage artificial intelligence and machine learning workloads, such as large language models and generative AI.

Microservices deployment: The scalability, fault tolerance, and service discovery capabilities of Kubernetes make it an essential tool for implementing microservices systems.

Hybrid/multi-cloud management: Kubernetes' capacity to unify cloud and on-premises environments is well established, allowing for consistent workload management across hybrid or multicloud deployments.

Edge computing: Kubernetes use in edge computing is widely recognized for lowering latency and enabling IoT and real-time analytics via lightweight distributions like K3s.

CI/CD automation: Kubernetes integrates with CI/CD pipelines to automate building, testing, and deployment for both traditional and AI/ML workloads.

Cloud-native applications: Kubernetes is the foundation of cloud-native application development, offering scalability, mobility, and high availability across various cloud environments.

Summary

In this introductory chapter, we laid the groundwork for our Kubernetes journey.

We defined Kubernetes as an orchestrator that automates the complex task of running distributed containerized applications as well as explored a brief history, tracing K8s back to Google's internal Borg and Omega systems, explaining its enterprise-grade DNA. We also looked at the landscape, comparing K8s to Docker Swarm (simpler but less powerful) and understanding why K8s became the industry standard. And at the end, we reviewed the concept of containerization and examined the use cases from microservices to AI that make Kubernetes valuable.

In the next chapter, we will introduce Docker, the foundational containerization platform. We will explore the relationship between Docker and Kubernetes, learn the key differences between them, examine alternative container runtimes and image-building tools, and then walk through a hands-on installation of Docker on Ubuntu.

CHAPTER 2

Getting Started with Docker

Introduction

In the previous chapter, Kubernetes was introduced as the orchestrator that coordinates containers at scale. However, before Kubernetes can do anything useful, there must be containers to orchestrate. This is where Docker enters the picture. Docker became the catalyst that pushed containers from a niche technology used by large tech companies into a mainstream tool that developers and operations teams could adopt in their daily work.

This chapter focuses on building a solid understanding of Docker as a container platform. The aim is not to turn the reader into a Docker expert but to provide enough practical and conceptual knowledge to make sense of how Kubernetes interacts with container images and runtimes later on. Along the way, the chapter also introduces the surrounding ecosystem, such as the Open Container Initiative (OCI) and alternative runtimes and image builders, so that readers understand why Docker is not the only option available today and why Kubernetes evolved beyond a single runtime.

By the end of this chapter, Docker will no longer feel like a black box. Instead, readers will see it as one important piece in a broader, standards-based container landscape and will have completed a hands-on installation and basic validation on Ubuntu that can be reused throughout the book.

Objectives

By the end of this chapter, we will be able to

- Describe, in simple terms, what Docker is and how it differs from Kubernetes

- Explain how Docker fits into the container ecosystem, including the role of OCI and why standardized image and runtime formats matter

B. M. Sabatini, *Kubernetes for Absolute Beginners*, https://doi.org/10.1007/979-8-8688-2445-6_2

- Recognize the difference between a container runtime and an image-building tool, and how Docker combines both

- Identify several alternative container runtimes and image builders and understand at a high level when they might be used

- Install Docker on an Ubuntu-based virtual machine using the official repositories

- Verify a Docker installation by pulling images, running containers, and validating connectivity to a sample web application

- Understand baseline resource considerations for running Docker on a virtual machine, avoiding configurations that are too constrained for practical use

Brief History of Docker and the Open Container Initiative

Docker did not start as a generic container engine. It emerged from the need to simplify packaging and shipping applications in a repeatable way. Before Docker, teams frequently struggled with the classic "works on my machine" problem, where applications behaved differently between development, testing, and production environments due to inconsistent dependencies and configurations.

Docker popularized the idea of treating an application and its dependencies as a single, portable unit that could run almost anywhere with minimal friction. Early versions of Docker bundled several responsibilities into one product: image building, image distribution, and container runtime. This all-in-one experience helped it grow rapidly in the developer community and made containers accessible beyond specialized infrastructure teams.

As adoption increased, it became clear that tying container standards to a single vendor would limit interoperability and slow innovation. To address this, major industry players created the Open Container Initiative (OCI). The OCI defines open standards for container image formats and runtime behavior. In practice, this means that a container image built by one tool can be executed by another runtime, as long as both follow the OCI specifications.

This shift was important for platforms like Kubernetes. Instead of depending on a single vendor-specific runtime, Kubernetes can use the OCI specifications along with the Container Runtime Interface (CRI) to integrate and manage different container runtimes. As a result, Docker became one important implementation in a much larger ecosystem, and other runtimes such as containerd and CRI-O could integrate cleanly without breaking existing workflows.

Today, when referring to Docker in the context of modern container platforms, it is helpful to think of it as one of several tools that implement open standards defined by OCI, rather than the only way to build and run containers.

Difference Between Docker and Kubernetes

When we speak about Kubernetes, it is worth mentioning what Docker is: it is a platform that simplifies the creation, deployment, and management of applications by using containers that are lightweight, portable units that package an application's code along with its dependencies and configurations. So far, Docker seems to have some clear similarities to Kubernetes; however, Kubernetes, on the other hand, is specifically a container orchestration tool designed to manage and automate the deployment, scaling, and operation of containers across a cluster of machines. This means that while Docker handles individual containers, Kubernetes excels at managing multiple containers at scale, offering features like load balancing, self-healing, and automated rollouts, as previously mentioned in the introduction chapter. They are complementary technologies often used together: Docker creates the containers, and Kubernetes orchestrates them in production environments (see Figure 2-1).

In this diagram, we compare the container runtime of Kubernetes and the building tool for images of Docker for managing containers. On the left, Kubernetes is shown using containerd as its container runtime, which directly manages the lifecycle of containers. Kubernetes orchestrates workloads across nodes, with containerd handling the low-level operations. On the right, Docker's architecture is depicted, where the Docker Engine uses BuildKit as its modern image-building tool to create container images efficiently. Therefore, both solutions eventually manage and execute containers, but Kubernetes specializes in large-scale orchestration, whereas Docker concentrates on standalone containerization and development workflows.

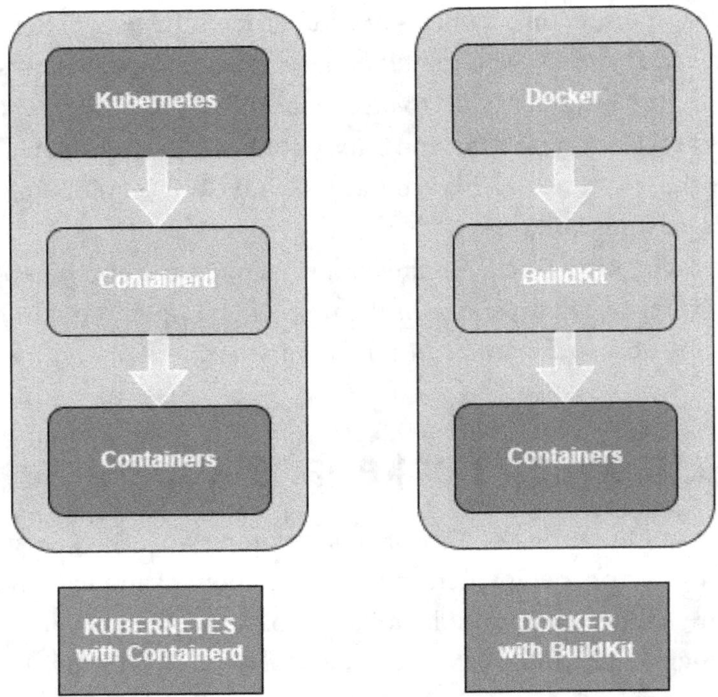

Figure 2-1. *Kubernetes vs. Docker BuildKit flows*

Table 2-1 illustrates the alternative runtime engine for Kubernetes.

Table 2-1. *Alternative container runtimes for Kubernetes*

Runtime	Short description
CRI-O	Kubernetes-specific runtime implementing the CRI standard for OCI containers.
Podman	Daemonless runtime with rootless security features; compatible with Docker CLI.
runC	Lightweight CLI tool adhering to OCI standards for running containers.
Kata Containers	Secure runtime using lightweight VMs for enhanced isolation.
LXC/LXD	OS-level virtualization offering full system containers with efficient resource use.
Singularity	HPC-focused runtime optimized for scientific computing environments.

And Table 2-2 illustrates the alternative tools for Docker.

Table 2-2. *Alternative image-building tools for Docker-compatible workflows*

Tool (Image builder)	Short description
Buildah	Daemonless tool for building OCI-compatible images; integrates well with Podman.
Kaniko	Builds container images inside Kubernetes clusters without privileged access.
Podman Build	Integrated build functionality within Podman for OCI-compliant images.
Skaffold	Automates builds and deployments for Kubernetes applications.
orca-build	Lightweight tool for building images without requiring privileged daemons.
umoci	Low-level tool for creating and modifying OCI-compliant images securely.

In this context, a shim is a thin compatibility layer that sits between two components to translate or adapt their communication. The Docker shim allowed Kubernetes to talk to the Docker Engine as if it were a native CRI implementation. When Kubernetes issued runtime-related requests, the shim converted those calls into the Docker-specific API. Removing the shim means Kubernetes now talks directly to runtimes that implement the CRI specification, reducing indirection and avoiding the need to maintain a special adapter.

Note   Kubernetes no longer integrates directly with the Docker Engine as a runtime. Instead, it communicates with container runtimes through the Container Runtime Interface (CRI). The former "Docker shim" acted as a compatibility layer between Kubernetes and Docker-specific APIs. Once the ecosystem had matured, CRI-compliant runtimes such as containerd and CRI-O made this shim unnecessary and was removed, simplifying the overall architecture and reducing maintenance overhead. The deprecation of the Docker shim happened in December 2020 and full removal in April 2022.

Understanding Dockerfiles

While using pre-built images from registries is convenient for learning and quick deployments, most real-world applications require customization beyond what base images provide. A Dockerfile is a text file containing a sequence of instructions that Docker uses to build a custom image from scratch or by extending an existing base image. Rather than manually installing dependencies and configuring environments inside containers, developers and operators define these steps declaratively in a Dockerfile, ensuring consistency and repeatability across all environments. Instructions such as RUN, COPY, and ADD create new filesystem layers, while others add metadata, all of which Docker caches to optimize rebuild times when only certain instructions change. Understanding how to write effective Dockerfiles is essential for leveraging Docker's full potential, as it shifts from simply running existing containers to creating reproducible, version-controlled application packaging that can be stored, shared, and deployed reliably across teams and infrastructure.

1. **Docker Installation**

    Now we will proceed to install Docker in our virtual machine that is running Ubuntu server, and then we will pull an image from Docker Hub, and at the end, we will run a container with this image and verify that it is running.

    Therefore, for the purpose of this installation and all future installations in this book, we will be using the Linux distribution Ubuntu. Consequently, please do keep in mind that for different operating systems we will need to use other commands, and we must consult the official web pages from Docker and Kubernetes to obtain the most updated commands [1]. Additionally, in order to execute these commands, we must have the sudo password of our Ubuntu machine.

Also, take into consideration that from now on in this book, all the commands will be run in a virtual machine on VMware Workstation Player 16 that is running the operating system Ubuntu 24.04.2 LTS. This operating system can be downloaded for free from the official website of Ubuntu, while if we do not have VMware Workstation Player 16, we can use any other open-source hypervisor.

When running Docker inside a virtual machine, it is important to allocate sufficient CPU and memory resources. While Docker itself is relatively lightweight, the containers we run will require additional capacity. For the examples in this book, a virtual machine with at least 2 virtual CPUs and 4 GB of RAM is recommended as a practical minimum. This allows the Docker engine, the underlying operating system, and one or more sample containers, such as a web server, to coexist without constant memory pressure or CPU starvation. Configurations with only 1 GB of memory tend to be too constrained and can lead to slow performance, frequent swapping, and unpredictable behavior when pulling images or running multiple containers at the same time.

Note   I recommend running the same commands from the official Docker repository.

This one and the next five commands are necessary to add Docker's official GPG key (see Figures 2-2, 2-3, 2-4, and 2-5).

```
sudo apt-get update
```

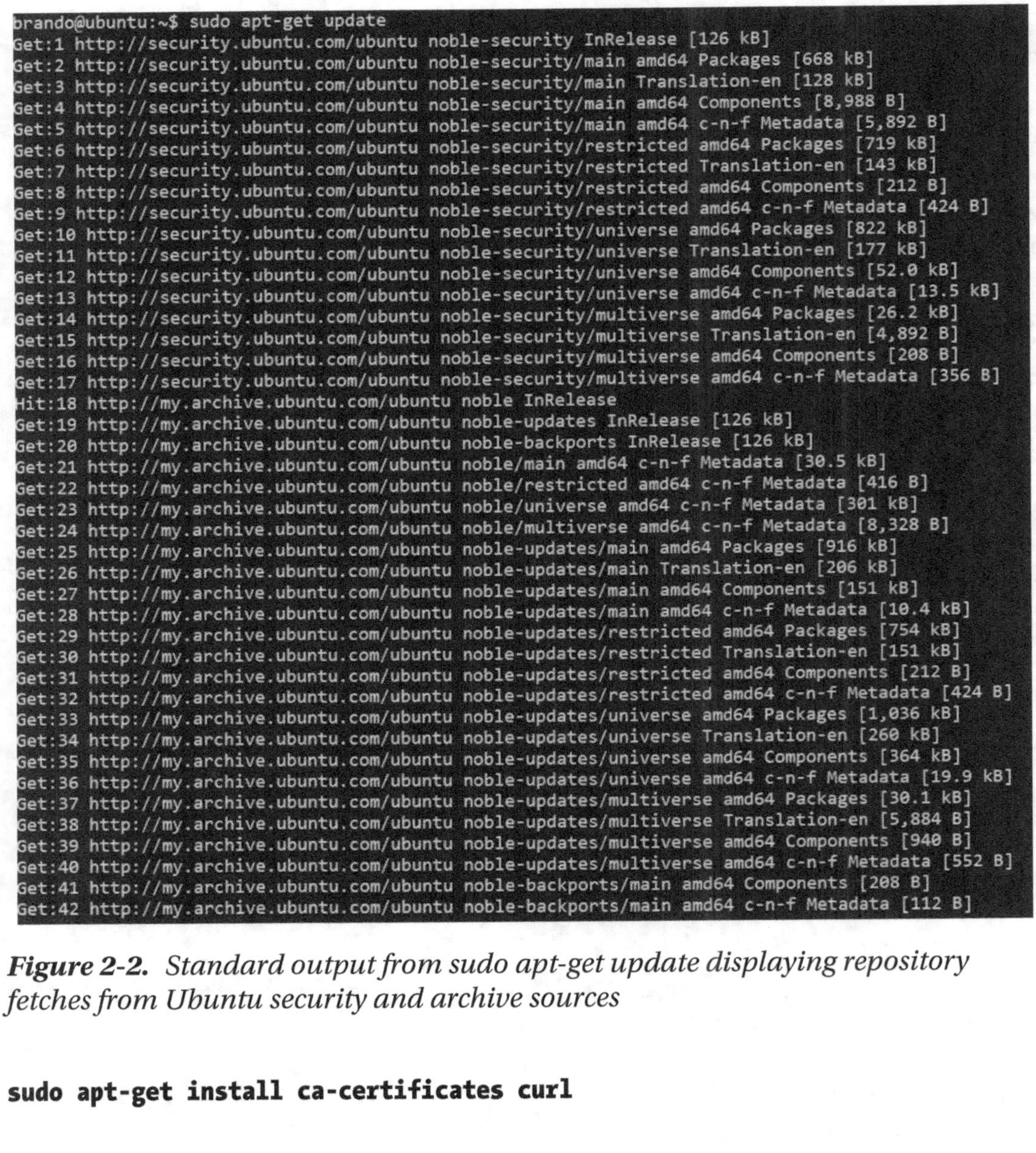

```
brando@ubuntu:~$ sudo apt-get update
Get:1 http://security.ubuntu.com/ubuntu noble-security InRelease [126 kB]
Get:2 http://security.ubuntu.com/ubuntu noble-security/main amd64 Packages [668 kB]
Get:3 http://security.ubuntu.com/ubuntu noble-security/main Translation-en [128 kB]
Get:4 http://security.ubuntu.com/ubuntu noble-security/main amd64 Components [8,988 B]
Get:5 http://security.ubuntu.com/ubuntu noble-security/main amd64 c-n-f Metadata [5,892 B]
Get:6 http://security.ubuntu.com/ubuntu noble-security/restricted amd64 Packages [719 kB]
Get:7 http://security.ubuntu.com/ubuntu noble-security/restricted Translation-en [143 kB]
Get:8 http://security.ubuntu.com/ubuntu noble-security/restricted amd64 Components [212 B]
Get:9 http://security.ubuntu.com/ubuntu noble-security/restricted amd64 c-n-f Metadata [424 B]
Get:10 http://security.ubuntu.com/ubuntu noble-security/universe amd64 Packages [822 kB]
Get:11 http://security.ubuntu.com/ubuntu noble-security/universe Translation-en [177 kB]
Get:12 http://security.ubuntu.com/ubuntu noble-security/universe amd64 Components [52.0 kB]
Get:13 http://security.ubuntu.com/ubuntu noble-security/universe amd64 c-n-f Metadata [13.5 kB]
Get:14 http://security.ubuntu.com/ubuntu noble-security/multiverse amd64 Packages [26.2 kB]
Get:15 http://security.ubuntu.com/ubuntu noble-security/multiverse Translation-en [4,892 B]
Get:16 http://security.ubuntu.com/ubuntu noble-security/multiverse amd64 Components [208 B]
Get:17 http://security.ubuntu.com/ubuntu noble-security/multiverse amd64 c-n-f Metadata [356 B]
Hit:18 http://my.archive.ubuntu.com/ubuntu noble InRelease
Get:19 http://my.archive.ubuntu.com/ubuntu noble-updates InRelease [126 kB]
Get:20 http://my.archive.ubuntu.com/ubuntu noble-backports InRelease [126 kB]
Get:21 http://my.archive.ubuntu.com/ubuntu noble/main amd64 c-n-f Metadata [30.5 kB]
Get:22 http://my.archive.ubuntu.com/ubuntu noble/restricted amd64 c-n-f Metadata [416 B]
Get:23 http://my.archive.ubuntu.com/ubuntu noble/universe amd64 c-n-f Metadata [301 kB]
Get:24 http://my.archive.ubuntu.com/ubuntu noble/multiverse amd64 c-n-f Metadata [8,328 B]
Get:25 http://my.archive.ubuntu.com/ubuntu noble-updates/main amd64 Packages [916 kB]
Get:26 http://my.archive.ubuntu.com/ubuntu noble-updates/main Translation-en [206 kB]
Get:27 http://my.archive.ubuntu.com/ubuntu noble-updates/main amd64 Components [151 kB]
Get:28 http://my.archive.ubuntu.com/ubuntu noble-updates/main amd64 c-n-f Metadata [10.4 kB]
Get:29 http://my.archive.ubuntu.com/ubuntu noble-updates/restricted amd64 Packages [754 kB]
Get:30 http://my.archive.ubuntu.com/ubuntu noble-updates/restricted Translation-en [151 kB]
Get:31 http://my.archive.ubuntu.com/ubuntu noble-updates/restricted amd64 Components [212 B]
Get:32 http://my.archive.ubuntu.com/ubuntu noble-updates/restricted amd64 c-n-f Metadata [424 B]
Get:33 http://my.archive.ubuntu.com/ubuntu noble-updates/universe amd64 Packages [1,036 kB]
Get:34 http://my.archive.ubuntu.com/ubuntu noble-updates/universe Translation-en [260 kB]
Get:35 http://my.archive.ubuntu.com/ubuntu noble-updates/universe amd64 Components [364 kB]
Get:36 http://my.archive.ubuntu.com/ubuntu noble-updates/universe amd64 c-n-f Metadata [19.9 kB]
Get:37 http://my.archive.ubuntu.com/ubuntu noble-updates/multiverse amd64 Packages [30.1 kB]
Get:38 http://my.archive.ubuntu.com/ubuntu noble-updates/multiverse Translation-en [5,884 B]
Get:39 http://my.archive.ubuntu.com/ubuntu noble-updates/multiverse amd64 Components [940 B]
Get:40 http://my.archive.ubuntu.com/ubuntu noble-updates/multiverse amd64 c-n-f Metadata [552 B]
Get:41 http://my.archive.ubuntu.com/ubuntu noble-backports/main amd64 Components [208 B]
Get:42 http://my.archive.ubuntu.com/ubuntu noble-backports/main amd64 c-n-f Metadata [112 B]
```

Figure 2-2. Standard output from sudo apt-get update displaying repository fetches from Ubuntu security and archive sources

```
sudo apt-get install ca-certificates curl
```

```
brando@ubuntu:~$ sudo apt-get install ca-certificates curl
Reading package lists... Done
Building dependency tree... Done
Reading state information... Done
ca-certificates is already the newest version (20240203).
ca-certificates set to manually installed.
curl is already the newest version (8.5.0-2ubuntu10.6).
curl set to manually installed.
0 upgraded, 0 newly installed, 0 to remove and 56 not upgraded.
```

Figure 2-3. *Shows the sudo apt-get install ca-certificates curl output with the latest manual versions*

```
sudo install -m 0755 -d /etc/apt/keyrings

sudo curl -fsSL \
  https://download.docker.com/linux/ubuntu/gpg \
  -o /etc/apt/keyrings/docker.asc

sudo chmod a+r /etc/apt/keyrings/docker.asc
```

```
brando@ubuntu:~$ sudo install -m 0755 -d /etc/apt/keyrings
brando@ubuntu:~$ sudo curl -fsSL https://download.docker.com/linux/ubuntu/gpg -o /etc/apt/keyrings/d
brando@ubuntu:~$ sudo chmod a+r /etc/apt/keyrings/docker.asc
```

Figure 2-4. *Downloading and sudo chmod for Docker GPG key file*

```
echo
"deb [arch=$(dpkg --print-architecture)
signed-by=/etc/apt/keyrings/docker.asc]
https://download.docker.com/linux/ubuntu
$(. /etc/os-release && echo "${UBUNTU_CODENAME:-$VERSION_CODENAME}")
stable" | sudo tee /etc/apt/sources.list.d/docker.list > /dev/null

sudo apt-get update
```

```
brando@ubuntu:~$ echo \
>     "deb [arch=$(dpkg --print-architecture) signed-by=/etc/apt/keyrings/docker.asc] https://download.docker.com/linux/ubuntu \
>     $(. /etc/os-release && echo "${UBUNTU_CODENAME:-$VERSION_CODENAME}") stable" | \
>     sudo tee /etc/apt/sources.list.d/docker.list > /dev/null
brando@ubuntu:~$ sudo apt-get update
Get:1 https://download.docker.com/linux/ubuntu noble InRelease [48.8 kB]
Get:2 https://download.docker.com/linux/ubuntu noble/stable amd64 Packages [20.3 kB]
Hit:3 http://security.ubuntu.com/ubuntu noble-security InRelease
Hit:4 http://my.archive.ubuntu.com/ubuntu noble InRelease
Hit:5 http://my.archive.ubuntu.com/ubuntu noble-updates InRelease
Hit:6 http://my.archive.ubuntu.com/ubuntu noble-backports InRelease
Fetched 69.2 kB in 1s (59.5 kB/s)
Reading package lists... Done
```

Figure 2-5. *Shows the deb [arch=amd64 signed-by=/etc/apt/keyrings/docker.asc] Docker repository line added*

```
sudo apt-get install \
  docker-ce docker-ce-cli containerd.io \
  docker-buildx-plugin docker-compose-plugin
```

```
brando@ubuntu:~$ sudo apt-get install docker-ce docker-ce-cli containerd.io docker-buildx-plugin docker-compose-plugin
Reading package lists... Done
Building dependency tree... Done
Reading state information... Done
The following additional packages will be installed:
  docker-ce-rootless-extras libltdl7 libslirp0 pigz slirp4netns
Suggested packages:
  cgroupfs-mount | cgroup-lite
The following NEW packages will be installed:
  containerd.io docker-buildx-plugin docker-ce docker-ce-cli docker-ce-rootless-extras docker-compose-plugin libltdl7 libslirp0 pigz slirp4netns
0 upgraded, 10 newly installed, 0 to remove and 56 not upgraded.
Need to get 120 MB of archives.
After this operation, 438 MB of additional disk space will be used.
Do you want to continue? [Y/n] Y
Get:1 https://download.docker.com/linux/ubuntu noble/stable amd64 containerd.io amd64 1.7.25-1 [29.6 MB]
5% [Connecting to my.archive.ubuntu.com] [1 containerd.io 7,077 kB/29.6 MB 24%]
```

Figure 2-6. *Shows the sudo apt-get install docker-ce docker-ce-cli containerd.io docker-buildx-plugin docker-compose-plugin confirmation prompt*

Now that the installation is complete (see Figure 2-6), we will run the command necessary to verify if Docker is currently running.

```
sudo docker run hello-world
```

Note   As we can see in Figure 2-7, Docker was not running, and therefore, the command triggered the action to find the Docker image locally. However, this image was not present on the OS, and consequently, it proceeded to retrieve the latest image from the online repository, and when the pull was completed and the image downloaded, the command was re-run automatically, and the output ended with "Hello from Docker!".

```
brando@ubuntu:~$ sudo docker run hello-world
Unable to find image 'hello-world:latest' locally
latest: Pulling from library/hello-world
e6590344b1a5: Pull complete
Digest: sha256:bfbb0cc14f13f9ed1ae86abc2b9f11181dc50d779807ed3a3c5e55a6936dbdd5
Status: Downloaded newer image for hello-world:latest

Hello from Docker!
This message shows that your installation appears to be working correctly.

To generate this message, Docker took the following steps:
 1. The Docker client contacted the Docker daemon.
 2. The Docker daemon pulled the "hello-world" image from the Docker Hub.
    (amd64)
 3. The Docker daemon created a new container from that image which runs the
    executable that produces the output you are currently reading.
 4. The Docker daemon streamed that output to the Docker client, which sent it
    to your terminal.

To try something more ambitious, you can run an Ubuntu container with:
 $ docker run -it ubuntu bash

Share images, automate workflows, and more with a free Docker ID:
 https://hub.docker.com/

For more examples and ideas, visit:
 https://docs.docker.com/get-started/

brando@ubuntu:~$
```

Figure 2-7. *Successful sudo docker run hello-world test output confirming Docker installation*

With this command, we can check the installed Docker version.

docker --version

While with this command, we can display the system-wide Docker configuration and resource usage (see Figure 2-8).

sudo docker info

With this command, we are going to pull the image of nginx, the latest one, from Docker Hub to have it locally in our machine (see Figure 2-9).

sudo docker pull nginx:latest

```
brando@ubuntu:~$ docker --version
Docker version 28.0.1, build 068a01e
brando@ubuntu:~$ sudo docker info
Client: Docker Engine - Community
 Version:    28.0.1
 Context:    default
 Debug Mode: false
 Plugins:
  buildx: Docker Buildx (Docker Inc.)
    Version:  v0.21.1
    Path:     /usr/libexec/docker/cli-plugins/docker-buildx
  compose: Docker Compose (Docker Inc.)
    Version:  v2.33.1
    Path:     /usr/libexec/docker/cli-plugins/docker-compose

Server:
 Containers: 2
  Running: 0
  Paused: 0
  Stopped: 2
 Images: 1
 Server Version: 28.0.1
 Storage Driver: overlay2
  Backing Filesystem: extfs
  Supports d_type: true
  Using metacopy: false
  Native Overlay Diff: true
  userxattr: false
 Logging Driver: json-file
 Cgroup Driver: systemd
 Cgroup Version: 2
 Plugins:
  Volume: local
  Network: bridge host ipvlan macvlan null overlay
  Log: awslogs fluentd gcplogs gelf journald json-file local splunk syslog
 Swarm: inactive
 Runtimes: io.containerd.runc.v2 runc
 Default Runtime: runc
 Init Binary: docker-init
 containerd version: bcc810d6b9066471b0b6fa75f557a15a1cbf31bb
 runc version: v1.2.4-0-g6c52b3f
 init version: de40ad0
 Security Options:
```

Figure 2-8. *Docker info output showing version 28.0.3 and configuration details*

```
brando@ubuntu:~$ sudo docker pull nginx:latest
latest: Pulling from library/nginx
7cf63256a31a: Pull complete
bf9acace214a: Pull complete
513c3649bb14: Pull complete
d014f92d532d: Pull complete
9dd21ad5a4a6: Pull complete
943ea0f0c2e4: Pull complete
103f50cb3e9f: Pull complete
Digest: sha256:9d6b58feebd2dbd3c56ab5853333d627cc6e281011cfd6050fa4bcf2072c9496
Status: Downloaded newer image for nginx:latest
docker.io/library/nginx:latest
```

Figure 2-9. *Shows the sudo docker pull nginx:latest layers download progress and completion*

With this command, we can run the image that we pulled previously.

```
sudo docker run -d -p 8080:80 nginx
```

While with this command, we can check the current running containers.

```
sudo docker ps
```

And with this command, we can test the access to the containerized web server (see Figure 2-10). The output is an HTML response, which typically starts with the structure of a simple web page rather than plain XML.

```
curl localhost:8080
```

```
brando@ubuntu:~$ sudo docker run -d -p 8080:80 nginx
970b5d92acf4688058568219835c59a8ad4b68f8c3f5fb4b6e51f79e1e350bec
brando@ubuntu:~$ sudo docker ps
CONTAINER ID    IMAGE       COMMAND             CREATED         STATUS         PORTS
                            NAMES
970b5d92acf4    nginx       "/docker-entrypoint.…"   10 seconds ago  Up 9 seconds   0.0.0.0:8080->80/t
cp, [::]:8080->80/tcp    brave_jackson
brando@ubuntu:~$ curl localhost:8080
<!DOCTYPE html>
<html>
<head>
<title>Welcome to nginx!</title>
<style>
html { color-scheme: light dark; }
body { width: 35em; margin: 0 auto;
font-family: Tahoma, Verdana, Arial, sans-serif; }
</style>
</head>
<body>
<h1>Welcome to nginx!</h1>
<p>If you see this page, the nginx web server is successfully installed and
working. Further configuration is required.</p>

<p>For online documentation and support please refer to
<a href="http://nginx.org/">nginx.org</a>.<br/>
Commercial support is available at
<a href="http://nginx.com/">nginx.com</a>.</p>

<p><em>Thank you for using nginx.</em></p>
</body>
</html>
brando@ubuntu:~$
```

Figure 2-10. *Shows the sudo docker run -d -p 8080:80 nginx output with container status and curl localhost:8080 welcome page*

Summary

We have now completed the Docker installation and the action to run our first container on Docker with the image nginx.

In this chapter, Docker was introduced as the foundational container platform that prepares the ground for Kubernetes. The chapter began by clarifying the relationship between Docker and Kubernetes: Docker focuses on building and running individual containers, while Kubernetes orchestrates many containers across clusters of machines. A brief historical perspective showed how Docker popularized containers and how the Open Container Initiative helped standardize image and runtime formats, allowing the ecosystem to evolve beyond a single vendor.

The chapter then contrasted Kubernetes container runtimes and Docker's image-building capabilities, highlighting how modern platforms rely on OCI-compliant runtimes such as containerd and CRI-O. Alternative runtimes and image-building tools were presented to show that organizations can choose the components that best fit their security, performance, and operational requirements.

On the practical side, a complete Docker installation on Ubuntu was performed, including configuring official repositories, installing the required packages, and validating the setup by running containers like hello-world and nginx. Along the way, resource considerations for the virtual machine were discussed, ensuring that the environment is realistic and stable for everyday use.

In the next chapter, the focus shifts from individual containers and the Docker engine to the core building blocks of a Kubernetes cluster. The control plane, worker nodes, Pods, and Services will be explored in detail, and a lightweight Kubernetes distribution (K3s) will be installed to demonstrate how these concepts come together in a working cluster.

Reference

[1]   Ubuntu (2025). Install Docker Engine on Ubuntu. Retrieved from
       https://docs.docker.com/engine/install/ubuntu/

CHAPTER 3

Understanding Kubernetes Basics

Introduction

We now have context about what Kubernetes is and its journey from Google's internal systems to the open-source standard it is today. But knowing the history and purpose is only part of the picture. To actually use Kubernetes effectively, we must understand how it is organized internally—the building blocks and the mechanisms that allow it to do what it does.

In this chapter, we will examine the structural foundations that form every Kubernetes deployment. We will see how clusters are assembled from different types of nodes, how the control plane makes decisions while remaining separate from the machines that execute work, and how Pods serve as the fundamental units that contain our applications. We will study the relationships between these components and gain a clear mental model of how a Kubernetes system actually operates. This understanding will prepare us to install a real cluster, deploy applications to it, and begin working with Kubernetes in practice.

Objectives

By the end of this chapter, we will be able to

- Describe how Kubernetes manages containerized applications through clusters and worker nodes

- Understand the roles of the control plane and worker nodes in orchestrating workloads

B. M. Sabatini, *Kubernetes for Absolute Beginners*, https://doi.org/10.1007/979-8-8688-2445-6_3

- Define Pods as the smallest deployable unit and explain how containers share resources within a Pod

- Explain the relationship between Nodes, Pods, and the overall cluster architecture

- Recognize how Kubernetes maintains the desired state and handles failures automatically

- Install and verify a basic Kubernetes cluster using K3s

- Deploy and test a simple application on a working Kubernetes cluster

Before we dive into Kubernetes basics, let's set the stage. For those of us just starting out, Kubernetes performs like an intelligent supervisor, overseeing our entire container operation. Imagine this: It manages clusters (groups of machines), which host Pods (groups of containers), ensuring our applications run like clockwork. Kubernetes automatically schedules where our apps run and uses a set of controllers that continuously compare the actual state of our cluster to the desired state, making adjustments as needed. While Kubernetes provides powerful mechanisms for scaling applications, automatic scaling—such as increasing or decreasing the number of running Pods in response to demand—requires explicit configuration through resources like the HorizontalPodAutoscaler or VerticalPodAutoscaler. Without these configurations, workloads will not scale automatically. But here's a tip: always ensure our cluster has enough spare capacity to scale; otherwise, we might face resource allocation errors or scheduling failures when expanding our applications, especially after hours.

Control Plane and Worker Nodes

Let's start with the basics we must know: a Node is a physical or virtual machine that provides the computational resources (CPU, memory, storage) needed to run Pods. Here's what's happening under the hood: every Node runs three critical components— the Kubelet, which communicates with the Kubernetes control plane to ensure Pods are running as specified; a container runtime (such as containerd) responsible for executing containers; and kube-proxy, which manages network rules to enable communication between Pods and external traffic. Additionally, remember this: nodes are pooled into clusters, letting Kubernetes distribute workloads across multiple machines for fault tolerance and scalability. The control plane (e.g., the API server, scheduler) dynamically assigns Pods to Nodes based on resource availability and constraints.

Alternatively, organizations can deploy Kubernetes on private infrastructure using solutions like OpenStack, which provides a foundation for managing clusters without relying on external cloud providers. This approach gives us full control over our infrastructure while maintaining the flexibility to run Kubernetes clusters.

Pods

Now we'll proceed to Pods, which are a group of one or more tightly coupled containers that share resources and operate like building blocks. Containers within a Pod share the same network namespace, meaning they use the same IP address and port space, enabling communication via localhost. They also share storage volumes, simplifying data exchange between co-located containers. All containers in a Pod are co-scheduled, running on the same Node and managed as a unified unit. While single-container Pods are the most common (acting as wrappers for individual applications), multi-container Pods are used for components that require close coordination, such as a primary application and its logging or monitoring sidecar. It is important to remember that Pods are temporary by design; if they fail or crash, Kubernetes automatically replaces them to maintain the desired state of our application. However, whether a Pod is automatically replaced after failure depends on how it was created—specifically, whether it's managed by a controller like a Deployment or running standalone. If a Pod is managed by a controller such as a Deployment, ReplicaSet, or StatefulSet, Kubernetes will automatically create a new Pod to maintain the desired state. In contrast, standalone Pods that are not managed by a controller will not be automatically recreated if they fail or are deleted. Within a running Pod, kubelet may restart individual containers according to the Pod's restartPolicy (which defaults to Always), but this only applies to container restarts within the same Pod instance, not to replacement of the Pod itself, which only happens when the Pod is managed by a controller such as a Deployment, ReplicaSet, or StatefulSet.

The interaction between Pods and Nodes occurs because Kubernetes schedules Pods on Nodes, with each Node hosting multiple Pods that use resources. Kubernetes recognizes when a node malfunctions or becomes unavailable and reschedules the impacted pods to nodes that are in good health. Because of that, this abstraction allows developers to focus on application logic while Kubernetes handles infrastructure complexities, ensuring reliability and scalability across distributed systems.

Kubernetes clusters follow a consistent architecture: a control plane orchestrates the cluster by managing the API server, scheduler, and controller manager, while one or more worker nodes execute the actual workloads. Deploying a Kubernetes cluster involves initializing the control plane first—which handles cluster state and decisions—then joining worker nodes to the cluster through secure token-based authentication. This separation ensures resilience, as control plane failures can be mitigated through high-availability configurations across multiple machines.

Kubernetes Cluster

Now, we will describe the main components of the Kubernetes cluster, which consists of at least one control plane and one or more worker Nodes (see Table 3-1).

Table 3-1. *Core Kubernetes Components, definitions of fundamental Kubernetes elements from the cluster level down to individual containers*

Component	Description
Cluster	It is a set of Nodes running containerized applications managed by Kubernetes.
Node	It is a physical or virtual machine within a cluster that runs Pods.
Pod	It is the smallest deployable unit in Kubernetes; it encapsulates one or more containers that share resources.
Container	A lightweight runtime environment for applications, isolated from other containers.
Control Plane	The software components that manage Kubernetes clusters, such as the API server, scheduler, and controller manager.
Worker Nodes	These machines are responsible for running application workloads.

Let's take a closer look at the Kubernetes architecture together (see Figure 3-1). For those of us who are just getting started, think of this diagram as our roadmap to understanding how all the pieces fit together in Kubernetes. We'll start from the top and work our way down so we can see how everything connects.

At the very top, we have the concept of a cluster. If we remember from earlier, a cluster is basically the main unit in Kubernetes, like a group of machines (which can be physical or virtual) working together to run our applications. Inside this cluster, we have two main types of Nodes: Control plane and Worker Nodes.

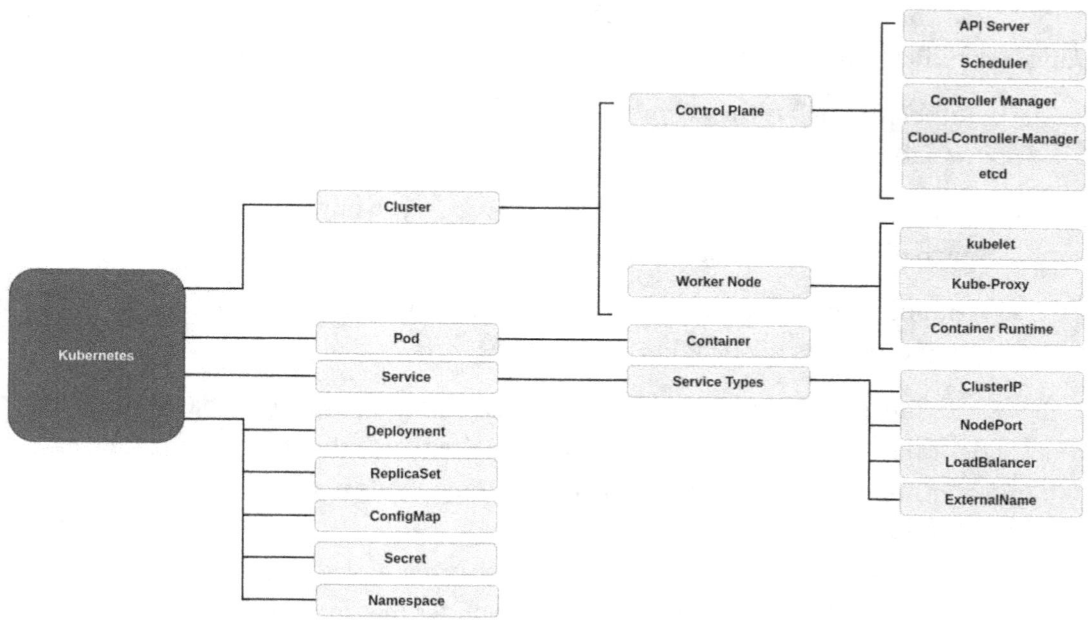

Figure 3-1. *Kubernetes Cluster Architecture, a comprehensive view of how the control plane manages the cluster, worker nodes execute workloads, and API objects define the desired state*

The Control plane is like the brain of the operation. It's where all the big decisions happen. Here, we'll find the Control Plane, which is made up of a few essential components:

- The API Server is our main point of contact. Whenever we (or any tool) want to talk to the cluster, we go through the API Server.

- The Scheduler is somehow like the traffic controller; it decides which Node should run which workload.

- The Controller Manager keeps an eye on things and makes sure everything matches the desired state we've set.

- The Cloud-Controller-Manager extends Kubernetes with cloud provider capabilities; it automates the setup of cloud resources such as load balancers and storage volumes that Kubernetes needs to function properly in environments like AWS, Azure, or GCP.

- And then there's etcd, which is basically the safe place to store all the important cluster data and settings.

25

Next, we have the Worker Nodes. These are the machines that actually do the heavy lifting by running our applications. Each Worker Node has a few key parts:

- Kubelet, which is the agent that makes sure our Pods are running the way they should

- Kube-Proxy, which handles all the networking so our apps can talk to each other (and the outside world) without a hitch

- And the Container Runtime, which is the engine that actually runs our containers inside Pods

Now, let's talk about Pods. If we've been following along, we know that Pods are the smallest deployable units in Kubernetes. Think of them as little warehouses that can hold one or more containers (our actual applications). Pods make it easy for containers to share resources and communicate.

But how do these Pods communicate with each other or with the outside world? That's where Services come in. Services are like friendly guides that make sure traffic gets to the right Pod, even if the Pods are moving around or being replaced. Kubernetes has different types of Services like ClusterIP, NodePort, LoadBalancer, and ExternalName, each with its own way of exposing our applications, either inside the cluster or to the outside world.

On top of that, Kubernetes introduces higher-level objects like Deployments and ReplicaSets. These help us scale our applications up or down and make sure the right number of Pods are always running.

Then, for managing configuration and sensitive data, Kubernetes gives us ConfigMaps and Secrets. And if we want to keep things organized or separate different teams or projects, Namespaces have us covered.

Basic Overview of Kubernetes

Here's a simplified diagram that gives us the big picture of Kubernetes architecture (see Figure 3-2). Imagine the Control Plane as the brain of Kubernetes; it's in charge of organizing, scheduling, and monitoring everything in the cluster. The Control Plane manages a bunch of Nodes (which are just machines, either physical or virtual), and each Node hosts Pods. Pods are the smallest units we can deploy in Kubernetes, and they hold one or more containers. Inside those containers, our actual applications are running. This setup shows how Kubernetes brings everything together to run and manage our apps efficiently, no matter where they're hosted.

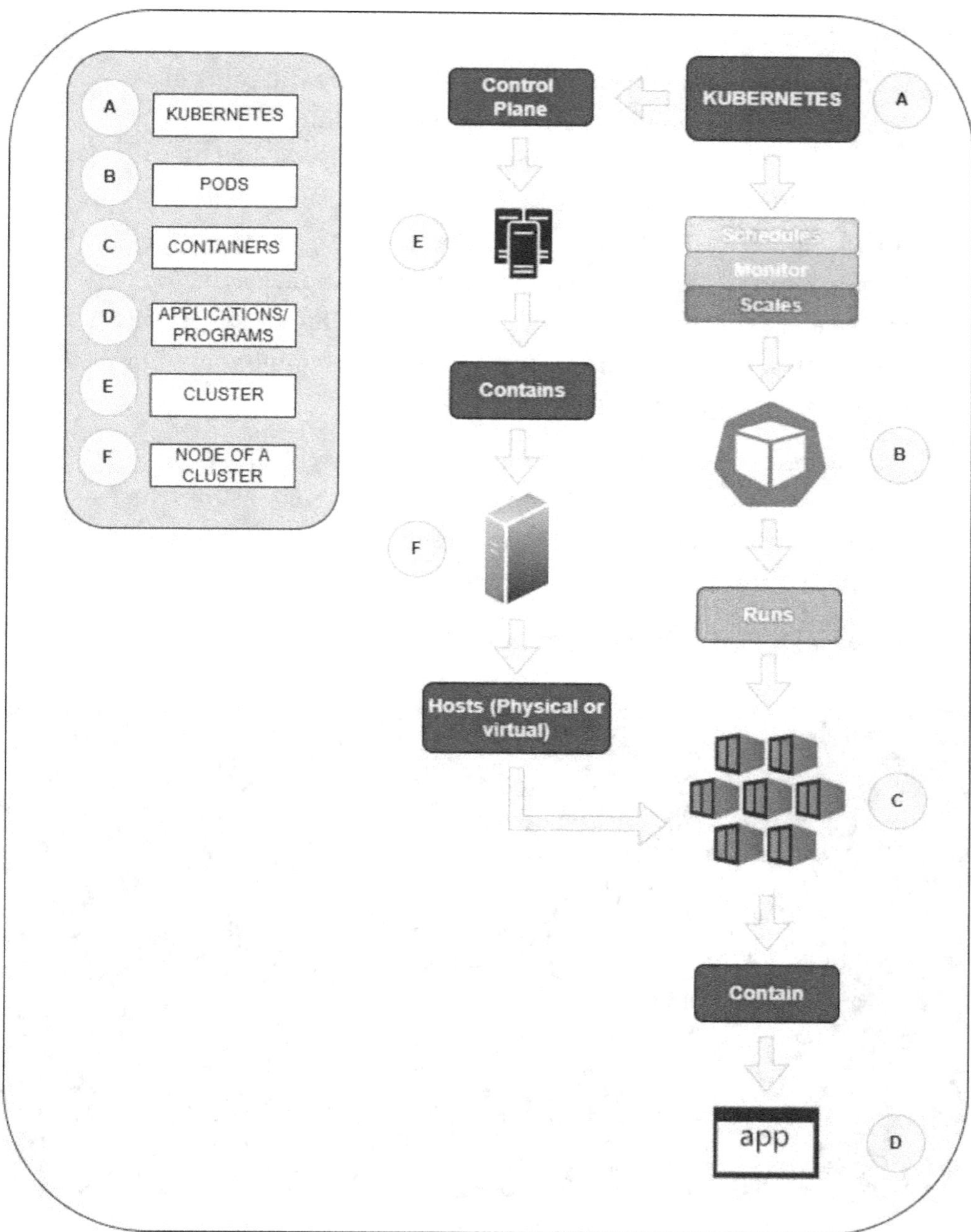

Figure 3-2. *Kubernetes Deployment Hierarchy, from the Kubernetes control plane down to containerized applications running on physical or virtual hosts*

1. **Installation of K3s**

   K3s is a lightweight version of Kubernetes that we can think of
   as Kubernetes stripped down to its essentials. Unlike the full
   Kubernetes distribution, K3s bundles everything we need into
   a single binary, making it much quicker to install and easier
   on system resources. This makes K3s perfect for us when we're
   learning, testing, or running Kubernetes on edge devices where
   we have limited computing power. The main difference: with full
   Kubernetes, we'd spend hours setting up all the components, but
   with K3s, we get a working cluster in seconds.

   For the purpose of understanding the basic concepts of
   Kubernetes, we will proceed with the installation of K3s from the
   official website. For this installation, we will use a single VM with
   the OS Ubuntu server.

```
sudo curl -sfL https://get.k3s.io | sh -
```

```
root@ubuntu:/home/brando# curl -sfL https://get.k3s.io | sh -
[INFO]  Finding release for channel stable

curl: (7) Failed to connect to github.com port 443 after 2095 ms: Couldn't connect to server
[INFO]  Using v1.32.3+k3s1 as release
[INFO]  Downloading hash https://github.com/k3s-io/k3s/releases/download/v1.32.3+k3s1/sha256sum-amd64.txt
[INFO]  Downloading binary https://github.com/k3s-io/k3s/releases/download/v1.32.3+k3s1/k3s
[INFO]  Verifying binary download
[INFO]  Installing k3s to /usr/local/bin/k3s
[INFO]  Skipping installation of SELinux RPM
[INFO]  Creating /usr/local/bin/kubectl symlink to k3s
[INFO]  Creating /usr/local/bin/crictl symlink to k3s
[INFO]  Skipping /usr/local/bin/ctr symlink to k3s, command exists in PATH at /usr/bin/ctr
[INFO]  Creating killall script /usr/local/bin/k3s-killall.sh
[INFO]  Creating uninstall script /usr/local/bin/k3s-uninstall.sh
[INFO]  env: Creating environment file /etc/systemd/system/k3s.service.env
[INFO]  systemd: Creating service file /etc/systemd/system/k3s.service
[INFO]  systemd: Enabling k3s unit
Created symlink /etc/systemd/system/multi-user.target.wants/k3s.service → /etc/systemd/system/k3s.service.
[INFO]  systemd: Starting k3s
root@ubuntu:/home/brando#
```

Figure 3-3. *Shows the bootkube downloading the Kubernetes release*

This downloads and runs the K3s installation script (see Figure 3-3). And then this
script sets up everything we need, like the Kubernetes control plane, the container
runtime, and even the kubectl command line tool. So, the installation takes a few
seconds. And when it's done, K3s will be running as a service on our VM.

2. **Checking If It Is Running Properly**

   Now we make sure everything is running properly with this command
   (see Figure 3-4).

   `sudo systemctl status k3s`

   (Press spacebar to scroll through the output or "q" to exit.)

```
root@ubuntu:/home/brando# sudo systemctl status k3s
● k3s.service - Lightweight Kubernetes
     Loaded: loaded (/etc/systemd/system/k3s.service; enabled; preset: enabled)
     Active: active (running) since Wed 2025-04-30 19:52:52 UTC; 2min 25s ago
       Docs: https://k3s.io
    Process: 2491 ExecStartPre=/bin/sh -xc ! /usr/bin/systemctl is-enabled --quiet nm-cloud-setup.s>
    Process: 2493 ExecStartPre=/sbin/modprobe br_netfilter (code=exited, status=0/SUCCESS)
    Process: 2495 ExecStartPre=/sbin/modprobe overlay (code=exited, status=0/SUCCESS)
   Main PID: 2497 (k3s-server)
      Tasks: 117
     Memory: 1.4G (peak: 1.4G)
        CPU: 4min 22.722s
     CGroup: /system.slice/k3s.service
             ├─2497 "/usr/local/bin/k3s server"
             ├─2547 "containerd "
             ├─3230 /var/lib/rancher/k3s/data/9c5025828cb319b4b3aed5bd59ed36df271b889c6ce6206e39e8a>
             ├─3288 /var/lib/rancher/k3s/data/9c5025828cb319b4b3aed5bd59ed36df271b889c6ce6206e39e8a>
             ├─3295 /var/lib/rancher/k3s/data/9c5025828cb319b4b3aed5bd59ed36df271b889c6ce6206e39e8a>
             ├─4385 /var/lib/rancher/k3s/data/9c5025828cb319b4b3aed5bd59ed36df271b889c6ce6206e39e8a>
             └─4547 /var/lib/rancher/k3s/data/9c5025828cb319b4b3aed5bd59ed36df271b889c6ce6206e39e8a>

Apr 30 19:54:31 ubuntu k3s[2497]: I0430 19:54:31.107090     2497 shared_informer.go:320] Caches are >
Apr 30 19:54:38 ubuntu k3s[2497]: I0430 19:54:38.134774     2497 pod_startup_latency_tracker.go:104]>
Apr 30 19:54:38 ubuntu k3s[2497]: I0430 19:54:38.223890     2497 event.go:389] "Event occurred" obje>
Apr 30 19:54:48 ubuntu k3s[2497]: I0430 19:54:48.246037     2497 replica_set.go:679] "Finished synci>
Apr 30 19:54:48 ubuntu k3s[2497]: I0430 19:54:48.390675     2497 event.go:389] "Event occurred" obje>
Apr 30 19:54:58 ubuntu k3s[2497]: I0430 19:54:58.151939     2497 range_allocator.go:247] "Successful>
Apr 30 19:54:59 ubuntu k3s[2497]: I0430 19:54:59.294718     2497 pod_startup_latency_tracker.go:104]>
Apr 30 19:54:59 ubuntu k3s[2497]: I0430 19:54:59.409873     2497 replica_set.go:679] "Finished synci>
Apr 30 19:54:59 ubuntu k3s[2497]: I0430 19:54:59.425092     2497 replica_set.go:679] "Finished synci>
Apr 30 19:54:59 ubuntu k3s[2497]: I0430 19:54:59.427035     2497 event.go:389] "Event occurred" obje>
lines 1-30/30 (END)...skipping...
● k3s.service - Lightweight Kubernetes
     Loaded: loaded (/etc/systemd/system/k3s.service; enabled; preset: enabled)
     Active: active (running) since Wed 2025-04-30 19:52:52 UTC; 2min 25s ago
       Docs: https://k3s.io
    Process: 2491 ExecStartPre=/bin/sh -xc ! /usr/bin/systemctl is-enabled --quiet nm-cloud-setup.ser\
    Process: 2493 ExecStartPre=/sbin/modprobe br_netfilter (code=exited, status=0/SUCCESS)
    Process: 2495 ExecStartPre=/sbin/modprobe overlay (code=exited, status=0/SUCCESS)
   Main PID: 2497 (k3s-server)
      Tasks: 117
     Memory: 1.4G (peak: 1.4G)
```

Figure 3-4. *Shows the successful kubelet systemd service enablement after the K3s server processes start*

3. **Using the Cluster**

   To start using the cluster, we can run this command that will
   automatically set up the kubectl cmd line for us.

   `sudo kubectl get nodes`

```
root@ubuntu:/home/brando# sudo kubectl get nodes
NAME       STATUS     ROLES                  AGE       VERSION
ubuntu     Ready      control-plane,master   6m20s     v1.32.3+k3s1
```

Figure 3-5. *Shows a single-node cluster ready after six minutes on v1.32.3+k3s1*

As we can see in Figure 3-5, the status is "Ready"; this means that it is working.

Now, to see in more detail what pods are running in the cluster, we can run this command.

sudo kubectl get pods --all-namespaces

```
root@ubuntu:/home/brando# sudo kubectl get pods --all-namespaces
NAMESPACE      NAME                                   READY   STATUS      RESTARTS   AGE
kube-system    coredns-ff8999cc5-pmz6j                1/1     Running     0          6m28s
kube-system    helm-install-traefik-crd-b48mf         0/1     Completed   0          6m27s
kube-system    helm-install-traefik-khtxz             0/1     Completed   2          6m27s
kube-system    local-path-provisioner-774c6665dc-kmdvc 1/1    Running     0          6m28s
kube-system    metrics-server-6f4c6675d5-j9b2d        1/1     Running     0          6m28s
kube-system    svclb-traefik-4e457341-d9bgl           2/2     Running     0          5m6s
kube-system    traefik-67bfb46dcb-4ktpf               1/1     Running     0          5m7s
root@ubuntu:/home/brando#
```

Figure 3-6. *Shows the kube-system pods running successfully*

In Figure 3-6, we can see that the previous kubectl command setup already has all that we need, like CoreDNS and metrics-server, etc.

4. **Test Deployment**

   Now, for testing purposes, we will try to run a simple web page.

   sudo kubectl create deployment hello-world --image=rancher/ hello-world

   This creates a tiny web application that just displays a "Hello World" message. To make it accessible, we run this command.

   sudo kubectl expose deployment hello-world --port=80 --type=NodePort

   Then, to check which port is in use, we can use this command.

   sudo kubectl get services hello-world

   And at the end, we can check with this command which pods are running (see Figure 3-7).

   sudo kubectl get pods

```
brando@ubuntu:~$ sudo kubectl create deployment hello-world --image=rancher/hello-world
deployment.apps/hello-world created
brando@ubuntu:~$ sudo kubectl expose deployment hello-world --port=80 --type=NodePort
service/hello-world exposed
brando@ubuntu:~$ sudo kubectl get services hello-world
NAME          TYPE        CLUSTER-IP     EXTERNAL-IP    PORT(S)        AGE
hello-world   NodePort    10.43.82.120   <none>         80:30254/TCP   12s
brando@ubuntu:~$ sudo kubectl get pods
NAME                          READY   STATUS             RESTARTS   AGE
hello-world-5b945cc466-q66rf  0/1     ContainerCreating  0          33s
brando@ubuntu:~$
```

Figure 3-7. *Shows the hello-world deployment and service exposure creation*

Note   For this book, we are using the official K3s commands and procedures
as provided by Rancher Labs (now part of SUSE) and documented in their official
guides [1].

Summary

In this chapter, we laid out the essential foundations of Kubernetes that every operator
must understand. We defined the Kubernetes cluster as a coordinated system of
machines working together, with the control plane making all the strategic decisions and
worker nodes executing the actual workloads. We explored Pods as the fundamental unit
of deployment, showing how they encapsulate containers and provide them with shared
networking and storage. We examined the architecture that separates control from
execution, allowing Kubernetes to remain resilient even when individual components
fail. We also walked through the core components—the control plane with its API server,
scheduler, and controller manager, along with the worker nodes running the kubelet,
container runtime, and kube-proxy—and understood how these pieces work together:
when we request to run an application, the scheduler places it intelligently, the kubelet
ensures it stays running, and controllers continuously compare what we want against
what actually exists, making corrections automatically. Finally, we gained practical
experience by installing K3s on a single virtual machine, verifying that our cluster was
operational, and deploying a test application to see these concepts in action.

In the next chapter, we will examine the Kubernetes architecture in detail, opening up the cluster to understand how the control plane components work together, how the scheduler makes decisions, how the controller manager maintains state, and how all these pieces communicate through APIs and protocols.

Reference

[1]   Rancher Labs (n.d.). K3s: Quick-start guide. Retrieved from `https://docs.k3s.io/quick-start`

CHAPTER 4

Kubernetes Architecture

Introduction

We now understand what Kubernetes does and the journey that brought it into existence. But understanding the what and the why is only half the story. The other crucial part is understanding how the internal design and organization allow Kubernetes to accomplish all those impressive feats.

Think of it this way: we might know that a ship requires a captain to steer it, but to truly appreciate how a ship operates across vast oceans, we need to understand its hull, its engines, its navigation systems, and how all these parts work together in harmony. The same applies to Kubernetes. Before we can confidently operate it, troubleshoot it, or make informed decisions about our deployments, we must grasp its structure.

In this chapter, we open the Kubernetes cluster and examine its core design. We will see how Kubernetes organizes itself into distinct functional areas, each with clear responsibilities. We will meet the components that decide where our applications run, the components that actually run them, and the components that ensure everything stays in the desired state. More importantly, we will understand why Kubernetes was designed this way and what benefits this architecture provides to us and our applications.

Objectives

By the end of this chapter, we will be able to

- Explain how Kubernetes separates management from execution through two distinct operational planes

- Identify the key components that make up the control plane and describe what each one does

© Brando Marzio Sabatini 2026

B. M. Sabatini, *Kubernetes for Absolute Beginners*, https://doi.org/10.1007/979-8-8688-2445-6_4

- Understand how worker nodes are organized and what runs on them to execute our workloads

- Trace the journey of a single pod creation request as it moves through the different components of a cluster

- Recognize how this architecture ensures that our applications remain resilient and continue running even when failures occur

- Appreciate the role of modern container runtimes and how they integrate with Kubernetes

Before exploring Kubernetes architecture, it is important to understand that this design forms the basis for how Kubernetes manages containerized applications at any scale. Kubernetes works as a distributed system, carefully built to ensure reliability, scalability, and operational efficiency for modern software environments.

Architecture Overview

Kubernetes divides its responsibilities between management and execution across two cooperating planes. The control plane is responsible for making decisions on the overall cluster state and responding to changes or events. Worker nodes, grouped in the data plane, actually run the application workloads and continuously report their status. This clear separation allows each side to scale independently. Problems affecting worker nodes do not disrupt the decisions made by the control plane, meaning applications can recover smoothly. In addition, this model allows Kubernetes to schedule applications across resources efficiently and isolates faults, so our workloads remain resilient (see Figure 4-1).

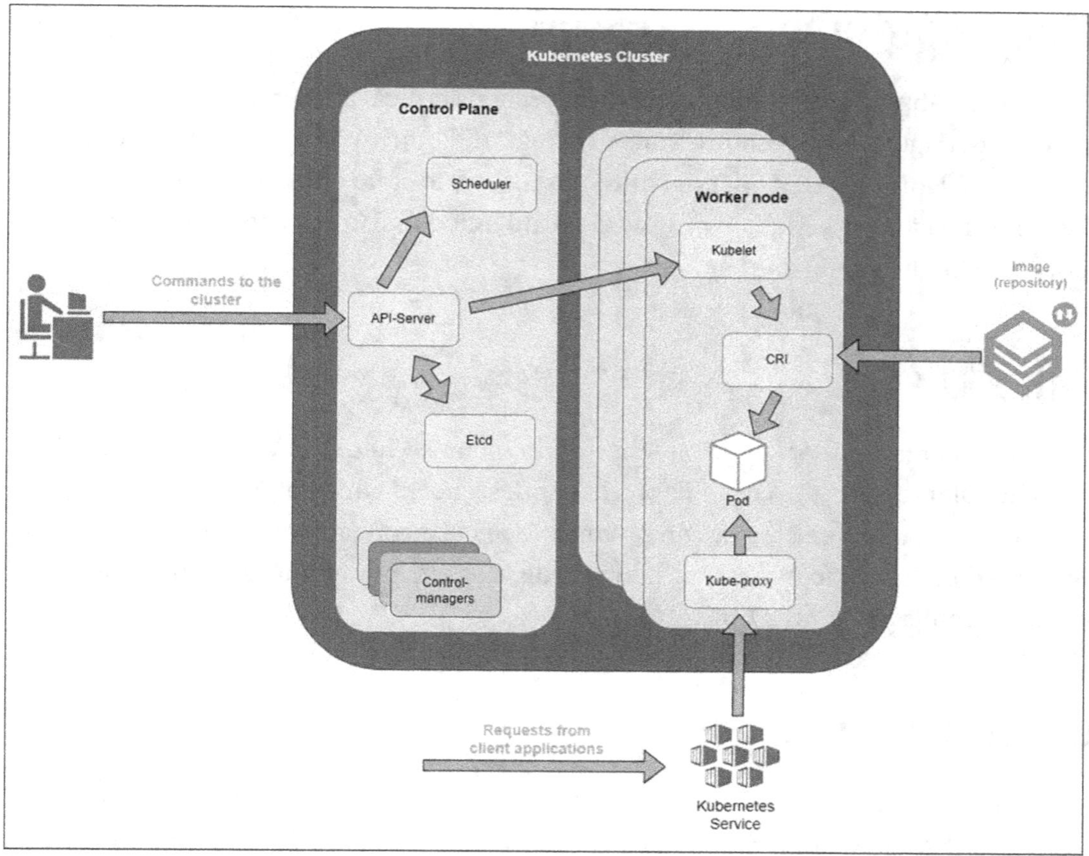

Figure 4-1. *Kubernetes cluster architecture*

Control Plane Components and the API Server

The control plane constantly works to keep the cluster in its desired state. At the heart of this is the API server. Every command or query, whether it comes from kubectl, controllers, or automated tools, is processed through the API server. This component checks every request for correctness and security, ensuring only valid and authorized actions make changes. When changes happen, the API server records these updates in etcd.

etcd: Distributed Data Store

etcd is a distributed key-value data store that retains critical cluster information. This includes configurations, resource states, secrets, and more. With its use of the Raft consensus algorithm, etcd offers a fault-tolerant way to store and access cluster data. Even if some etcd nodes fail, as long as most are functional, our cluster's memory remains reliable and up-to-date.

Scheduler

The scheduler is another key part of the control plane. When a new pod is requested, the scheduler reviews the available worker nodes, checks which ones match the pod's requirements, and then chooses an optimal node based on factors like resource use and affinity rules. This process ensures pods are distributed in ways that keep the cluster stable and efficient.

Controller Manager

The controller manager runs several controllers that make sure the cluster's actual state always matches the desired state described by the user. Each controller operates through a continuous cycle known as a control loop, which watches the cluster for changes and takes corrective action when needed. This cycle begins with observation, where the controller monitors resources and compares their current state against what was declared. When a discrepancy appears, the controller reconciles the difference by issuing commands to bring things back into alignment. If a pod fails or a node becomes unavailable, these controllers detect the issue and replace or reschedule pods automatically, keeping services online and healthy. Because each controller runs independently and asynchronously, multiple reconciliation processes can work simultaneously without interfering with one another. This design ensures that even if a controller temporarily fails, the cluster continues functioning, and when the controller restarts, it resumes its monitoring without losing track of the cluster's state.

Cloud Controller Manager

For those running Kubernetes in cloud environments, the cloud controller manager manages interactions with cloud providers. It takes care of specific tasks like provisioning load balancers, handling storage, or managing nodes. By separating cloud-specific logic, Kubernetes remains flexible across different environments.

Worker Node Components

Worker nodes are the machines assigned to run our actual applications. Each node has a kubelet, which ensures that assigned pods are launched and running as expected. Communication with the rest of the cluster happens through the container runtime interface, which allows different container runtimes (such as containerd or CRI-O) to work seamlessly with the kubelet.

Kubelet

Kubelet runs on every worker node to keep pods operating exactly as defined. It starts containers by pulling images when needed, checks their health using liveness and readiness probes, and communicates with the rest of the cluster through the container runtime interface. This constant monitoring helps maintain the desired state and ensures our applications stay responsive and reliable.

Container Runtime Interface

The container runtime interface, or CRI, is what allows Kubernetes to use different container runtimes on each node without needing to change any core Kubernetes code. It defines a standard way for the kubelet to communicate with the container runtime, such as containerd or CRI-O, handling tasks like pulling images, starting containers, and managing their lifecycle. By using CRI, Kubernetes gains both flexibility and consistency, making it easy to adapt to new runtimes as technology evolves.

Kube-proxy

On each worker node, kube-proxy is responsible for network management. It updates networking rules so that traffic is always routed to the right places, enabling service discovery within the cluster and balancing requests across pods as needed.

Component Interaction

Pod creation in Kubernetes follows a specific flow. When a new workload is requested, the API server first validates the request and stores it in etcd. The scheduler examines the cluster, picks a suitable worker node, and the node's kubelet launches the required containers. The controller manager monitors the process and reacts to problems, making sure the running applications always match the desired configuration. Kube-proxy ensures that the application can be reached and that network paths are maintained. At every stage, updates are recorded in etcd, supporting high reliability and consistency.

Modern Enhancements

In recent years, Kubernetes has improved its scalability, security, and efficiency. The container runtime interface has expanded support for new runtimes, letting users choose the best option for their needs. Stronger admission controls and advanced network policies have increased overall security. Cluster networking is now more capable and performant, handling workloads with demanding traffic needs.

Admission controllers have become especially important for adding security and consistency. They examine requests before any changes are recorded to the cluster, allowing organizations to enforce specific policies across clusters.

Production Considerations

For those preparing Kubernetes for production, building a highly available cluster is essential. This involves running multiple API server instances, distributing etcd across different nodes for durability, and ensuring controllers are backed up for redundancy. Storage is typically provided through distributed solutions or through dynamic provisioning with StorageClasses to keep data safe and accessible. Networking is carefully designed to combine high performance with security measures like encryption and network segmentation.

Procedures such as creating and restoring etcd backups can change between Kubernetes versions. Always refer to the latest official documentation for our specific version when planning for data protection and recovery.

Version Compatibility and Upgrade Scenarios

When planning cluster upgrades, understanding Kubernetes version compatibility is critical for maintaining system stability. Kubernetes maintains support for the three most recent minor versions, with each release cycle occurring approximately four months apart, resulting in three minor releases per calendar year. Before upgrading, it is essential to verify that our applications, container runtimes, and third-party components are compatible with the target version. Many critical features and APIs evolve between versions, and certain APIs may be deprecated or removed entirely. Testing upgrades in a staging environment that mirrors our production cluster is strongly recommended, ensuring that controllers, storage drivers, and network plugins continue functioning as expected. During rolling updates of cluster components, the control plane maintains backward compatibility for a limited period, allowing older clients to communicate with newer API servers. However, this grace period is temporary, and eventual full compatibility across all components is necessary. Organizations should establish a versioning strategy that aligns with their operational capacity and risk tolerance, keeping systems current while allowing adequate time for validation and planning.

Summary

Kubernetes separates the thinking from the doing. The control plane thinks, decides, and remembers. The worker nodes execute and report back. The API server validates every request, etcd stores all cluster state, the scheduler decides where pods run, and the controller manager continuously watches and corrects drift. On the worker nodes, the kubelet supervises containers, the container runtime interface connects to actual container engines, and kube-proxy handles networking.

What matters most is how these components work together. When we create a pod, the controller continuously watches it, the kubelet keeps it healthy, etcd records its state, and kube-proxy makes it reachable. If something fails, controllers automatically respond. This self-correcting loop is what makes Kubernetes resilient.

The next chapter takes each piece and explains how it actually works. We will explore the API server's request handling, etcd's role in storing cluster state, the scheduler's placement logic, and how controllers maintain desired state. We will also examine the kubelet, container runtimes, kube-proxy, and kubectl. By the end of Chapter 5, we will understand not just what these components do, but how to work with them directly.

Core Kubernetes Components

Introduction

In the previous chapter, we mapped out the overall architecture of Kubernetes, getting a high-level view of how clusters are organized. However, understanding the big picture is only the beginning. To truly work effectively with Kubernetes, we need to zoom in and examine each core component in detail, understanding not just what they are, but how they interact to deliver the resilience, automation, and scalability that make Kubernetes so powerful.

In this chapter, we'll explore the heart of the control plane and the essential processes that run on every node. We'll examine how the API server acts as the gatekeeper for all cluster operations, how etcd maintains the cluster's persistent state, how the scheduler intelligently places workloads, and how controllers keep everything running as we intend. We'll also look at the networking and storage abstractions that allow pods to communicate and persist data. By the end, we'll have a clear picture of each component's role and how they work together to orchestrate containerized applications.

Objectives

By the end of this chapter, we will be able to

- Understand the role of the API server as the central gateway for all cluster operations

- Explain how etcd stores and maintains the cluster's persistent state

© Brando Marzio Sabatini 2026

B. M. Sabatini, *Kubernetes for Absolute Beginners*, https://doi.org/10.1007/979-8-8688-2445-6_5

- Describe how the kube-scheduler decides which node should run each pod

- Identify how controllers maintain the desired state across the cluster

- Understand the kubelet's responsibility for node-level execution and container management

- Recognize the importance of networking components (kube-proxy, CNI) and DNS (CoreDNS) for pod communication

- Understand how kubectl serves as our command-line interface to the cluster

- Know the role of Container Network Interface (CNI) and Container Storage Interface (CSI) in the Kubernetes ecosystem

Control Plane Architecture

To understand how Kubernetes delivers on the promise of resilient, automated, and scalable container orchestration, it is essential to see its core components in context. While in Chapter 4 we mapped out the architecture, here we focus on what each main component does and how it behaves in a real cluster today. We proceed in the style of earlier chapters: unpacking each layer without fragmenting the learning journey (see Figure 5-1).

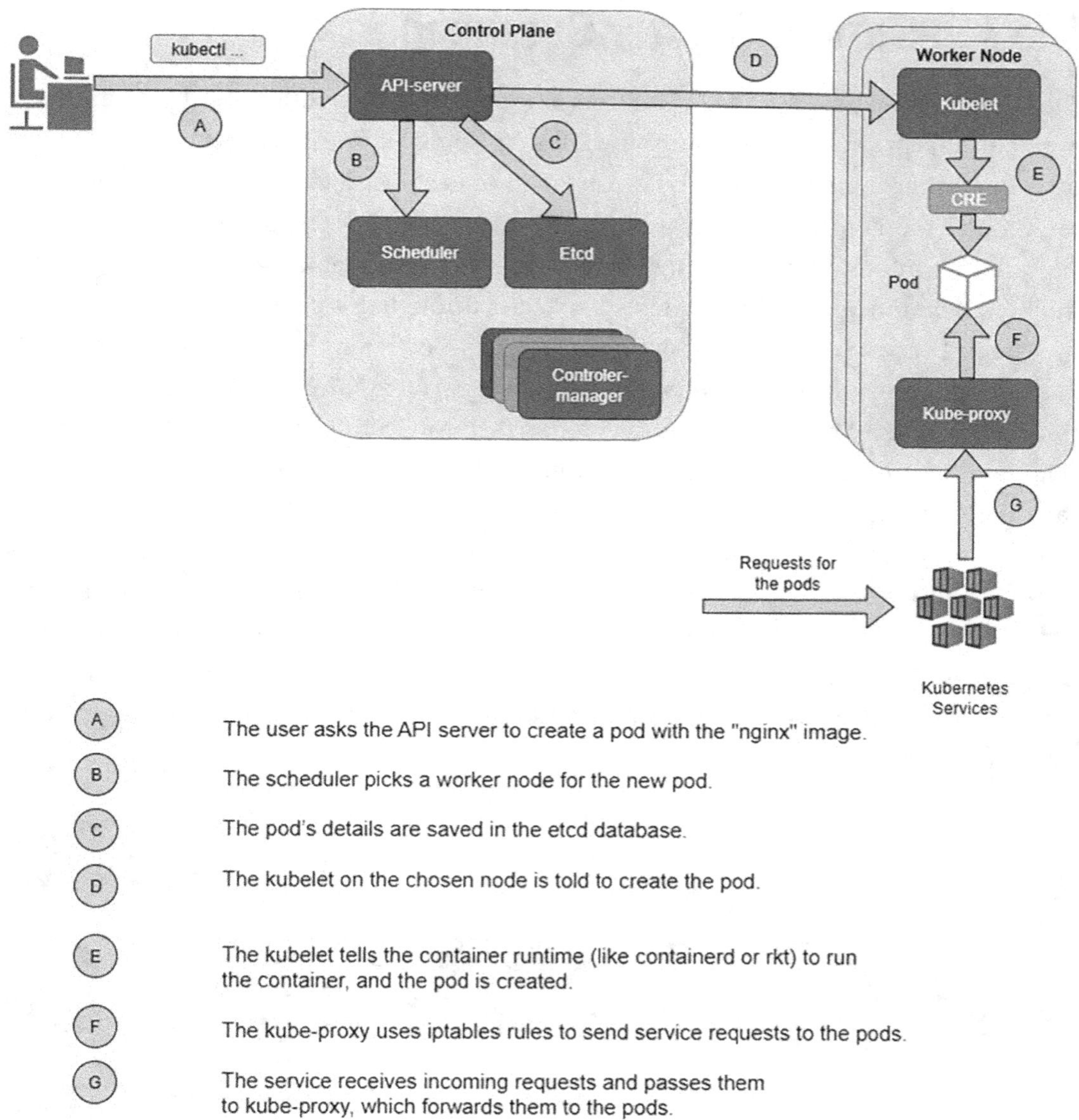

Figure 5-1. High-level overview of how a pod request travels from kubectl through the control plane to the worker node where the pod is created and exposed via services

The API Server: Cluster Gatekeeper

The control plane holds all the logic Kubernetes needs for scheduling and running workloads. Its primary components, the kube-apiserver, kube-scheduler, kube-controller-manager, and etcd, work together to steward the cluster. Whenever we use kubectl, our command addresses the API server, which is responsible for serving requests and interfacing with etcd, the persistent storage for all cluster state. All object creation, deletion, and listing requests must pass through this gatekeeper.

The API server processes common HTTP verbs. For example, when we retrieve pod status by running kubectl get pods, the API server performs an HTTP GET, fetching objects from etcd. The server supports modern security configurations: TLS 1.2 is the default minimum version, with TLS 1.3 available through explicit configuration using flags like --tls-min-version=VersionTLS13. While OAuth2 integration provides flexible authentication options through external identity providers, production clusters typically rely on Kubernetes' native authentication mechanisms, including client certificates, service account tokens, and webhook authentication. Issuing updates or deletions follows similar request routing—always through this central API interface. This means the API server provides auditability and validates every interaction before changing the cluster (see Figure 5-2).

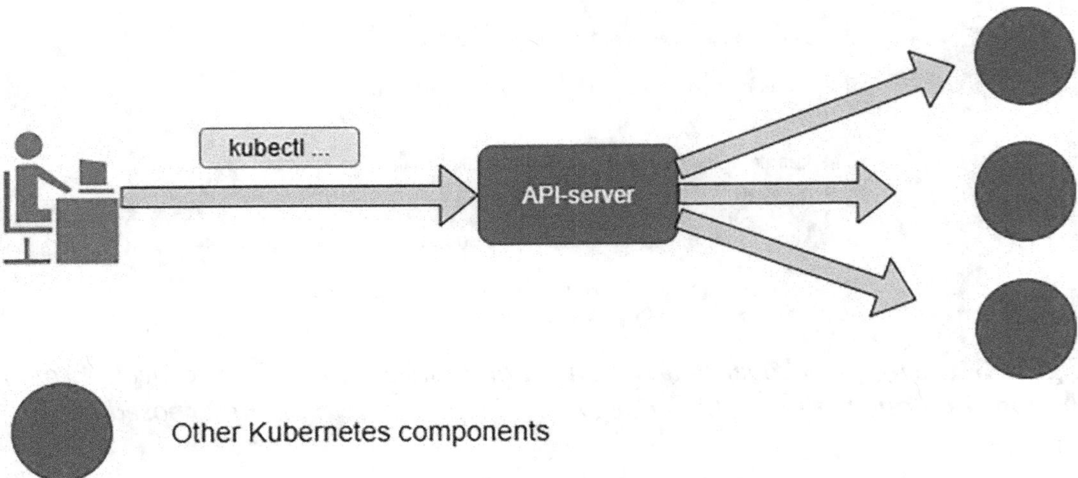

Figure 5-2. *Simplified view of how kubectl talks to the API server, which then fans out requests to the different Kubernetes components it manages*

etcd: The Cluster's Persistent Memory

etcd, forming the persistent "memory" of Kubernetes, stores every bit of cluster data: deployments, secrets, and service endpoints. Controllers rely on etcd for reliable state reflection. In 2025, etcd 3.6.0 marks a leap in efficiency: operations now scale smoothly even in large clusters because the allocation algorithm has been redesigned for constant time (O(1)) performance. This release also streamlines memory use, improves throughput on state updates, and reduces operational overhead. When etcd is set up, redundancy is achieved by running multiple nodes, continuously electing a leader to ensure consistency and high availability—details that, while abstracted away from basic hands-on management, crucially underpin all production use. Backups are straightforward: commands like etcdctl snapshot save are part of standard workflows and always recommended before upgrades or maintenance to safeguard cluster state.

The Scheduler: Intelligent Workload Placement

The kube-scheduler is the cluster's assignment engine. When a new Pod is created, the scheduler selects the node best suited to run it based on up-to-date resource accounting and request analysis. In real practice, workload placement isn't guesswork; it matches pod requirements for CPU and memory against node allocation, integrates advanced requirements for specialized hardware (like GPUs), and supports taints and tolerations. Dynamic Resource Allocation (DRA), which reached beta in Kubernetes 1.32 and continues evolving in 1.33, means that the scheduler can now handle fine-grained resources, such as exclusive devices, using declarative resource claims. The core DRA feature targets general availability in Kubernetes 1.34, marking a significant milestone for resource management. This evolution is especially meaningful for modern machine learning or analytics workloads, driving higher efficiency and reliability.

Controller Management: Maintaining Desired State

Controllers continuously observe actual versus desired state across the cluster. In daily operation, this translates to maintaining a target number of replicas, watching for pod or node failures, managing upgrades through rolling deployment strategies, and automatically replacing unhealthy elements. The ReplicaSet controller, DaemonSet controller, and Job controller all fall under the controller manager process, which tracks lifecycle events and issues corrective actions. If we scale a deployment, the ReplicaSet controller immediately launches or removes pods to match our specification, updating etcd accordingly.

The Kubelet: Node-Level Execution

The kubelet is the hands-on agent residing on every cluster node. Its role was introduced in the previous chapter; here, we clarify how it implements our intentions from the control plane. On receiving instructions, the kubelet ensures that containers are started, volumes are mounted, probes for liveness and readiness execute, and errors are reported upstream. All modern kubelets talk to a container runtime using standardized interfaces. Since Kubernetes 1.24 (May 2022), Docker is no longer used directly, with containerd or CRI-O taking over. The kubelet autonomously manages liveness and readiness checks, responding either by restarting unhealthy containers or marking them as unavailable to the cluster. The kubelet remains the fundamental process that executes pod specifications and reports node conditions back to the API server.

Network Connectivity: Service Routing and Discovery

Network connectivity is managed by kube-proxy. Each node runs this forwarder, managing the cluster's internal virtual networking. Requests to services are transparently routed by kube-proxy, with traffic directed to healthy pods according to service definitions. In a practical setup, when a service (for instance, a ClusterIP type) is created to front multiple pods, kube-proxy programs rules historically using iptables, with IPVS preferred for large-scale deployments due to its $O(1)$ computational complexity. The nftables backend, which reached general availability in Kubernetes 1.33, provides another modern option for network rule management. While iptables remains the default for compatibility, the shift toward modern network backends like IPVS and nftables enables lower latency and seamless scalability, supporting thousands of services even as clusters grow in size. Service discovery builds on this routing, with DNS names always mapping back to cluster-allocated IPs.

DNS Resolution: CoreDNS Integration

Managing DNS is handled by CoreDNS, integrated as the default Kubernetes DNS provider. CoreDNS provides automatic name resolution for services and pods so that distributed applications communicate using stable, DNS-based service names. When a service is deployed, CoreDNS instantly advertises its name (like nginx.default.svc.cluster. local), making pod connections reliable regardless of IP fluctuation. Misconfiguration or DNS failure is a common root cause of application connectivity problems and should be part of any troubleshooting checklist. In modern clusters, CoreDNS is highly configurable through plugins, monitoring metrics, resolving external names, and providing caching for high-throughput scenarios.

Kubectl

kubectl, though not running inside the cluster, remains the user's entry point. All tasks, like creating deployments, listing resources, and tailoring live objects, use this single command-line tool. Its subresources and plugin ecosystem offer workflows for all levels of administration, from quick state checks to advanced patching and rollouts.

A note on pronunciation: We will hear this tool called by many names in the industry. The official Kubernetes community pronunciation is "cube-control," as it controls the cluster. However, many engineers affectionately say "cube-cuddle" (as if hugging the cluster), while others stick to the literal "cube-c-t-l." All of these are widely understood, so we can feel free to use whichever one flows best for us.

The Role of the Container Network Interface (CNI)

Beyond the internal components like kube-proxy, we must also rely on a dedicated Network Plugin to establish the actual communication paths between our Pods. While kube-proxy creates the routing rules that make Services work, it is the CNI plugin that acts as the digital electrician, assigning unique IP addresses to every Pod and ensuring that data traffic can travel seamlessly between different worker nodes. Because Kubernetes is designed to be modular, it does not include a built-in solution for this Pod-to-Pod data transfer; instead, we install a CNI-compliant provider—such as Calico,

Flannel, or Cilium—to make the network functional. This separation allows us to choose a networking strategy that best fits our specific security or performance needs without modifying the core Kubernetes software.

Managing Storage with the Container Storage Interface (CSI)

We find this same modular approach when our applications need to save permanent data using the Container Storage Interface (CSI). The control plane components we have discussed are optimized for orchestration and scheduling, so they do not interact directly with physical hard drives or cloud storage arrays. Instead, they communicate with CSI drivers to provision and attach storage volumes to the worker nodes exactly when a workload requires them. By offloading these hardware-specific tasks to a standardized interface, we ensure that the Kubernetes control plane remains lightweight and stable while still retaining the flexibility to connect to any storage backend, from local disks to enterprise cloud storage systems.

Summary

In this chapter, we examined the core components that orchestrate Kubernetes: the API server as the central gatekeeper, etcd as persistent memory, the kube-scheduler for intelligent placement, and the controller manager maintaining desired state. We explored the kubelet's role on every node, kube-proxy, and CoreDNS for networking and service discovery, and kubectl as our command-line interface. These components, along with the modular CNI and CSI abstractions, work in harmony to deliver Kubernetes' core promise of automated, resilient, and scalable container orchestration.

In the next chapter, we will explore how we define workloads and configurations using YAML files.

CHAPTER 6

Working with YAML Files

Introduction

Welcome to mastering YAML configuration in Kubernetes. If we are picking up this chapter, we have explored the foundational architecture and container concepts that underpin Kubernetes. However, before we dive into commands and configuration management, it is vital to understand the context: How do we express our desired state to Kubernetes? What format does the system expect? And why has YAML become the standard language for infrastructure as code?

In this chapter, we will build our practical foundation for configuration management. We won't just examine syntax rules; we will explore how YAML serves as our primary communication mechanism with Kubernetes, how its structure translates intentions into deployable resources, and the kubectl workflows that transform our declarative configurations into running systems. This understanding will make every subsequent chapter about managing Deployments, Services, and stateful applications far easier to grasp.

Objectives

By the end of this chapter, we will be able to

- Understand YAML fundamentals and how its structure defines Kubernetes resource hierarchies

- Recognize core YAML syntax elements, including indentation, key-value pairs, lists, and comments

- Create practical Kubernetes manifests that define Pods and Deployments using declarative configuration

- Apply YAML files to our cluster using kubectl and verify deployment outcomes

© Brando Marzio Sabatini 2026
B. M. Sabatini, *Kubernetes for Absolute Beginners*, https://doi.org/10.1007/979-8-8688-2445-6_6

When working with Kubernetes, one of the most important and essential skills we'll need to master is creating and managing YAML files. YAML is a human-readable data format that has become the standard for defining Kubernetes resources. Essentially, YAML serves as the primary language for communicating our desired state to Kubernetes. While Kubernetes also accepts JSON format, YAML has become more popular due to its readability and simplicity.

Understanding YAML Basics

Before we jump into Kubernetes-specific YAML, it is essential that we first understand the basic structure and syntax of YAML files. YAML is designed to be human-readable and focuses on data representation rather than document markup. Its syntax is intentionally minimal, making it easier to read and write compared to formats like XML or even JSON.

Key YAML Syntax Elements

The foundation of YAML rests on a few simple principles. Indentation defines structure, where each level of nesting uses consistent spacing to show relationships between different elements. Key-value pairs form the basic building blocks, expressed as key: value combinations that can represent everything from simple configuration values to complex nested objects. Lists create sequences of related items using the hyphen character, perfect for defining multiple containers within a pod or several environment variables.

The YAML files are built using the fundamental elements given in Table 6-1.

Table 6-1. *Lists core YAML syntax for Kubernetes files*

Element	Description
Indentation	YAML uses spaces (not tabs) for indentation, typically two spaces per level. This indentation defines the structure and hierarchy of the data.
Key-value pairs	The basic building block of a YAML file is a key-value pair: `key: value`.

List/Arrays	Lists are created using hyphens:
	`fruits:`
	`- apple`
	`- orange`
	`- banana`

Maps/ Dictionaries	Nested structures are created using indentation:
	`person:`
	`name: John`
	`age: 30`

Comments	Comments begin with the `# character`.
Multiline Strings	For longer text, YAML provides several ways to handle multiline strings.

Creating Our First Kubernetes YAML File

Building upon our discussion of pods from the previous chapter, let's create a practical YAML file that defines a simple web server pod. This exercise demonstrates how declarative configuration translates abstract concepts into concrete deployments. We'll explore pods in much greater detail in Chapter 7: Managing Pods in Kubernetes, but this introduction will help us understand how YAML is used to define them.

Here's how to create our first pod using the nano text editor:

first-pod.yaml

```
apiVersion: v1
kind: Pod
metadata:
  name: first-pod
  labels:
    app: web-server
    environment: learning
spec:
  containers:
  - name: nginx-container
    image: nginx:1.25
    ports:
    - containerPort: 80
```

Save the file using Ctrl+O, then press Enter to confirm, and exit with Ctrl+X. This YAML file demonstrates several key concepts we've covered: the pod serves as the smallest deployable unit, metadata provides organizational information through labels, and the specification describes the desired state, including container images and network ports.

Applying YAML Files with kubectl

The kubectl apply command transforms our YAML declarations into running Kubernetes resources. This command represents the bridge between our desired state (expressed in YAML) and the actual cluster state managed by the control plane components we discussed earlier (see Figure 6-1).

```
sudo kubectl apply -f first-pod.yaml
```

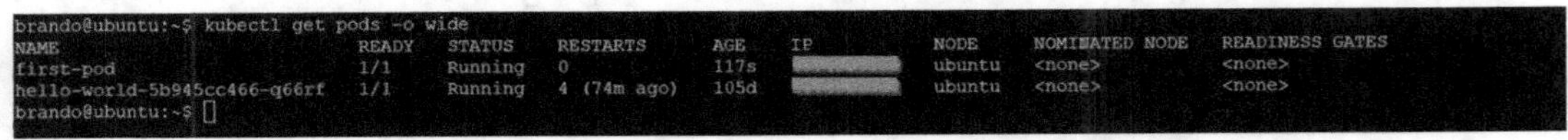

Figure 6-1. *Output from sudo kubectl apply -f first-pod.yaml shows the Pod named first-pod successfully created in the default namespace*

To verify our pod is running and see where Kubernetes scheduled it, use

```
kubectl get pods -o wide
```

The -o wide flag provides additional information including IP addresses and node assignments, helping us understand how Kubernetes scheduled our workload across the cluster.

Best Practices for Production Environments

As mentioned in previous chapters about scalability and automation, production Kubernetes environments require disciplined approaches to configuration management. Version control all YAML files to track changes and enable rollbacks when necessary. Use consistent naming conventions that clearly identify the purpose and environment of each resource, such as prefixing names with the application they belong to.

Separate environment-specific values from core configuration using ConfigMaps and Secrets rather than hardcoding values directly into YAML files. This approach, which we'll explore in detail in the ConfigMaps and Secrets chapter, enables the same YAML file to work across development, testing, and production environments with different configuration values.

Resource limits and requests should always be specified in production YAML files to ensure predictable scheduling and prevent resource contention. These specifications help the Kubernetes scheduler make informed decisions about pod placement across cluster nodes.

Practical Exercise

We'll create a Kubernetes deployment file step-by-step using the nano editor, turning a basic Pod into a robust Deployment.

Open the Editor and Create the File

```
nano web-deployment.yaml
```

This opens a new empty file in nano.

Here, we will write our Kubernetes Deployment configuration.

Start with the API Version and Kind

Type the first lines:

```
apiVersion: apps/v1
kind: Deployment
```

apiVersion: apps/v1 → This is the correct API group for deployments in modern Kubernetes versions.

kind: Deployment → Declares that we want a Deployment resource, not just a Pod.

Add Metadata

Right after those two lines, add an indented metadata section:

```
metadata:
  name: web-deployment
  labels:
    app: web
```

name is the unique name of our Deployment.

labels help group resources with a key-value pair—here, app: web.

Define the Specification of the Deployment

Underneath, start the spec block, where we control how the Deployment behaves:

```
spec:
  replicas: 3
  selector:
    matchLabels:
      app: web
```

replicas: 3 creates three Pods running this application.

selector.matchLabels ensures the Deployment manages only Pods labeled app: web.

Add the Pod Template

Still inside spec, define the pod's template:

```
template:
  metadata:
    labels:
      app: web
  spec:
    containers:
    - name: web-container
      image: nginx:latest
      ports:
      - containerPort: 80
```

Let's break it down:

template → This is the pod blueprint.

metadata.labels → Must match the selector.matchLabels above.

containers (list) → Defines one container in the Pod:

name: Logical name of the container (web-container).

image: Container image to run (nginx:latest).

ports: Opens port 80 inside the container for web traffic.

Full YAML File

Our web-deployment.yaml should now look like this:

web-deployment.yaml

```yaml
apiVersion: apps/v1
kind: Deployment
metadata:
  name: web-deployment
  labels:
    app: web
spec:
  replicas: 3
  selector:
    matchLabels:
      app: web
  template:
    metadata:
      labels:
        app: web
    spec:
      containers:
      - name: web-container
        image: nginx:latest
        ports:
        - containerPort: 80
```

Save and exit nano

Press CTRL+O → then Enter to save.

Press CTRL+X to exit nano.

Apply the Deployment to Kubernetes

Run

```
sudo kubectl apply -f web-deployment.yaml
```

Verify the Deployment

Check that it's running (see Figure 6-2):

```
kubectl get deployments
kubectl get pods -l app=web
```

```
brando@ubuntu:~$ kubectl apply -f web-deployment.yaml
deployment.apps/web-deployment created
brando@ubuntu:~$ kubectl get deployments
NAME              READY     UP-TO-DATE     AVAILABLE     AGE
hello-world       1/1       1              1             105d
web-deployment    0/3       3              0             12s
brando@ubuntu:~$ kubectl get pods -l app=web
NAME                              READY     STATUS      RESTARTS    AGE
web-deployment-5f9bb7d6b5-42n45   1/1       Running     0           28s
web-deployment-5f9bb7d6b5-ft77j   1/1       Running     0           28s
web-deployment-5f9bb7d6b5-v58bh   1/1       Running     0           28s
brando@ubuntu:~$ []
```

Figure 6-2. *Output from kubectl apply -f web-deployment.yaml confirms the web-deployment Deployment created with 3/3 Pods running and ready*

What Did We Do?

We have now transformed a single Pod into a scalable Deployment with three replicas.

Summary

In this chapter, we explored YAML as the primary language for expressing our desired state to Kubernetes. We examined the fundamental YAML syntax elements— indentation, key-value pairs, lists, and comments—that form the foundation of all Kubernetes configurations. We created practical examples demonstrating how YAML structure translates into Pods and Deployments, and we learned how kubectl apply bridges our declarative configurations with cluster reality.

In the next chapter, we will explore how to manage Pods in Kubernetes, building on the YAML skills we have just mastered. We'll examine pod lifecycle phases, troubleshooting techniques, and health monitoring capabilities that ensure our deployments remain stable and responsive in production environments.

CHAPTER 7

Managing Pods in Kubernetes

Introduction

Welcome to pod management in Kubernetes. If you are picking up this chapter, we have likely heard about the importance of managing Kubernetes pods, yet before we dive into commands, configurations, and troubleshooting, it is vital to understand the context: What are pods? How do they work? And why does their lifecycle matter?

In this chapter, we will build our practical foundation. We won't just look at definitions; we will explore the story of how pods function as Kubernetes' smallest deployable units, how they progress through lifecycle phases, and the kubectl commands that give us visibility into their behavior. This understanding will make every subsequent chapter about higher-level abstractions like Deployments and StatefulSets far easier to grasp.

Objectives

By the end of this chapter, we will be able to

- Understand pod fundamentals and why pods are ephemeral by design

- Recognize the five pod lifecycle phases and what each state reveals about pod status

© Brando Marzio Sabatini 2026
B. M. Sabatini, *Kubernetes for Absolute Beginners*, https://doi.org/10.1007/979-8-8688-2445-6_7

- Create pods using declarative YAML manifests following production best practices

- Use essential kubectl commands to monitor, inspect, and troubleshoot pod behavior

Before we dive into managing pods, let's build on what we've learned so far. In Chapter 4, we explored the Kubernetes architecture, and in Chapter 6, we mastered YAML configuration skills. Now we'll put it all together to understand how pods work as the smallest deployable units in Kubernetes. Think of pods as the bridge between your containerized applications and the cluster's orchestration capabilities. When you understand pod lifecycle management, you'll be able to harness the self-healing and scaling properties that make Kubernetes such a powerful platform for modern application deployment.

Understanding Pod Fundamentals

Let's start with what we need to know about pods. Pods represent Kubernetes' approach to grouping containers that need to work closely together, much like how we discussed container relationships in Chapter 2 with Docker. Each pod creates a shared execution environment where containers can communicate through localhost interfaces while maintaining the isolation benefits that containers provide. This design reflects the reality that many applications consist of multiple processes that need coordinated deployment and lifecycle management.

Here's something important to understand: pods are ephemeral by nature, which means they're temporary. This distinguishes them from traditional server management approaches. Rather than maintaining long-lived instances that require patching and updates, Kubernetes treats pods as disposable units that can be created, destroyed, and replaced as needed. When a pod fails, the system typically creates a fresh replacement rather than attempting repairs, ensuring consistency and reducing the complexity of state management.

While we focus on direct pod creation here, Deployments manage pods through ReplicaSets for stateless workloads, whereas StatefulSets maintain ordered deployment and stable identities for stateful applications, a distinction we'll explore in a later chapter. For now, this foundation in pod ephemeralness is essential to understanding why stateful services require the additional guarantees StatefulSets provide.

Now, let's look at pod lifecycle progression. Pods follow well-defined phases that provide visibility into deployment status:

- **Pending phase:** This occurs when pods have been accepted by the cluster but cannot yet start, often due to resource constraints or image pulling delays.

- **Running phase:** These pods have successfully started all containers, though this doesn't guarantee they're ready to serve traffic.

- **Succeeded phase:** This applies to pods that complete their work and exit cleanly, typically seen in batch processing scenarios.

- **Failed phase:** These pods indicate that one or more containers terminated with errors.

- **Unknown status:** This usually reflects communication problems between the control plane components we discussed in Chapter 5.

Creating and Managing Pod Deployments

Now we'll proceed to create pods in production environments. Pod creation typically occurs through declarative YAML configurations rather than imperative commands, following the patterns we established in Chapter 6. While commands like "**kubectl run nginx --image=nginx:1.21 --port=80**" work well for testing, YAML manifests provide the documentation and version control benefits that production deployments require.

Let's create a comprehensive pod specification that demonstrates essential configuration elements. We'll use the same workflow we established in previous chapters:

web-server-pod.yaml

We can create this pod using the same workflow we established in previous chapters:

```
nano web-server-pod.yaml
```

```
sudo kubectl apply -f web-server-pod.yaml
```

```
apiVersion: v1
kind: Pod
metadata:
  name: web-server-pod
  labels:
    app: nginx
    environment: production
    version: v1.21
spec:
  containers:
  - name: nginx-container
    image: nginx:1.21
    ports:
    - containerPort: 80
      name: http
    resources:
      requests:
        memory: "128Mi"
        cpu: "250m"
      limits:
        memory: "256Mi"
        cpu: "500m"
    env:
    - name: NGINX_PORT
      value: "80"
```

Essential Pod Management Operations

Let's explore the kubectl commands that help us monitor pod status and provide different levels of detail about pod behavior. We'll start with the basic commands and then move to a more detailed investigation.

The basic kubectl get pods command shows current status across the default namespace, while adding --all-namespaces provides cluster-wide visibility:

```
sudo kubectl get pods --all-namespaces -o wide
```

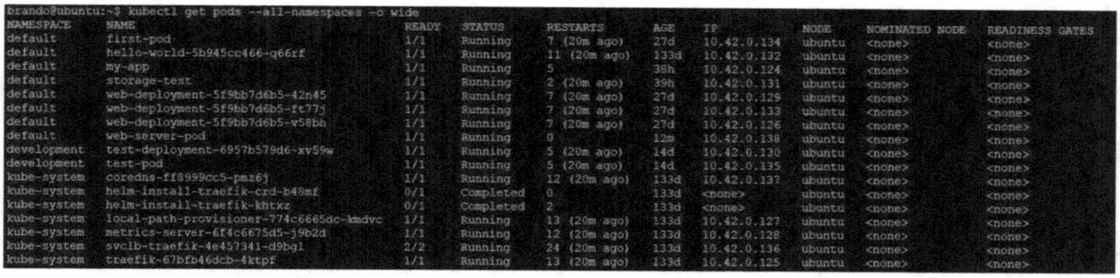

```
brando@ubuntu:~$ kubectl get pods --all-namespaces -o wide
NAMESPACE     NAME                                      READY   STATUS      RESTARTS        AGE    IP             NODE     NOMINATED NODE   READINESS GATES
default       first-pod                                 1/1     Running     7 (20m ago)     27d    10.42.0.134    ubuntu   <none>           <none>
default       hello-world-5b945cc466-q66rf              1/1     Running     11 (20m ago)    133d   10.42.0.132    ubuntu   <none>           <none>
default       my-app                                    1/1     Running     5               38h    10.42.0.124    ubuntu   <none>           <none>
default       storage-test                              1/1     Running     2 (20m ago)     39h    10.42.0.131    ubuntu   <none>           <none>
default       web-deployment-5f9bb7d6b5-42n45           1/1     Running     7 (20m ago)     27d    10.42.0.129    ubuntu   <none>           <none>
default       web-deployment-5f9bb7d6b5-ft77j           1/1     Running     7 (20m ago)     27d    10.42.0.133    ubuntu   <none>           <none>
default       web-deployment-5f9bb7d6b5-v58bh           1/1     Running     7 (20m ago)     27d    10.42.0.126    ubuntu   <none>           <none>
default       web-server-pod                            1/1     Running     0               12m    10.42.0.138    ubuntu   <none>           <none>
development   test-deployment-6957b579d6-xv59w          1/1     Running     5 (20m ago)     14d    10.42.0.130    ubuntu   <none>           <none>
development   test-pod                                  1/1     Running     5 (20m ago)     14d    10.42.0.135    ubuntu   <none>           <none>
kube-system   coredns-ff8999cc5-pmz6j                   1/1     Running     12 (20m ago)    133d   10.42.0.137    ubuntu   <none>           <none>
kube-system   helm-install-traefik-crd-b48mf            0/1     Completed   0               133d   <none>         ubuntu   <none>           <none>
kube-system   helm-install-traefik-khtxz                0/1     Completed   2               133d   <none>         ubuntu   <none>           <none>
kube-system   local-path-provisioner-774c6665dc-kmdvc   1/1     Running     13 (20m ago)    133d   10.42.0.127    ubuntu   <none>           <none>
kube-system   metrics-server-6f4c6675d5-j9b2d           1/1     Running     12 (20m ago)    133d   10.42.0.128    ubuntu   <none>           <none>
kube-system   svclb-traefik-4e457341-d9bgl              2/2     Running     24 (20m ago)    133d   10.42.0.136    ubuntu   <none>           <none>
kube-system   traefik-67bfb46dcb-4ktpf                  1/1     Running     13 (20m ago)    133d   10.42.0.125    ubuntu   <none>           <none>
```

Figure 7-1. *Output of the kubectl get pods command showing pod status, IP addresses, and node assignments*

Figure 7-1 shows this command reveals not just pod status but also IP addresses and node assignments, helping us understand how the scheduler distributed workloads across our cluster.

For detailed pod investigation, we use the describe command, which provides comprehensive information about configuration, events, and current state:

```
sudo kubectl describe pod web-server-pod
```

```
IP:   10.42.0.138
Containers:
  nginx-container:
    Container ID:   containerd://89d06a255c814874871a783c3268abb23b1fcc41b8a5e3c099bbc5ce2926aa81
    Image:          nginx:1.21
    Image ID:       docker.io/library/nginx@sha256:2bcabc23b45489fb0885d69a06ba1d648aeda973fae7bb981bafbb884165e514
    Port:           80/TCP
    Host Port:      0/TCP
    State:          Running
      Started:      Thu, 11 Sep 2025 11:08:09 +0000
    Ready:          True
    Restart Count:  0
    Limits:
      cpu:          500m
      memory:       256Mi
    Requests:
      cpu:          250m
      memory:       128Mi
    Environment:
      NGINX_PORT:   80
    Mounts:
      /var/run/secrets/kubernetes.io/serviceaccount from kube-api-access-j667s (ro)
Conditions:
  Type                        Status
  PodReadyToStartContainers   True
  Initialized                 True
  Ready                       True
  ContainersReady             True
  PodScheduled                True
Volumes:
  kube-api-access-j667s:
    Type:                    Projected (a volume that contains injected data from multiple sources)
    TokenExpirationSeconds:  3607
    ConfigMapName:           kube-root-ca.crt
    ConfigMapOptional:       <nil>
    DownwardAPI:             true
QoS Class:                   Burstable
Node-Selectors:              <none>
Tolerations:                 node.kubernetes.io/not-ready:NoExecute op=Exists for 300s
                             node.kubernetes.io/unreachable:NoExecute op=Exists for 300s
Events:
  Type     Reason     Age   From                Message
  ----     ------     ---   ----                -------
  Normal   Scheduled  12m   default-scheduler   Successfully assigned default/web-server-pod to ubuntu
  Normal   Pulling    12m   kubelet             Pulling image "nginx:1.21"
  Normal   Pulled     11m   kubelet             Successfully pulled image "nginx:1.21" in 15.52s (15.52s including waiting). Image size: 56746739 bytes.
  Normal   Created    11m   kubelet             Created container: nginx-container
  Normal   Started    11m   kubelet             Started container nginx-container
brando@ubuntu:~$
```

Figure 7-2. *Output of kubectl describe pod command displaying pod configuration, events, and current state*

As shown in Figure 7-2, the output includes scheduling decisions, resource allocation, and a chronological event history that proves invaluable during troubleshooting. Pay particular attention to the Events section, which shows the sequence of actions Kubernetes took when managing the pod.

We can access logs through kubectl to get direct insight into application behavior:

```
sudo kubectl logs web-server-pod
```

```
brando@ubuntu:~$ kubectl logs web-server-pod
/docker-entrypoint.sh: /docker-entrypoint.d/ is not empty, will attempt to perform configuration
/docker-entrypoint.sh: Looking for shell scripts in /docker-entrypoint.d/
/docker-entrypoint.sh: Launching /docker-entrypoint.d/10-listen-on-ipv6-by-default.sh
10-listen-on-ipv6-by-default.sh: info: Getting the checksum of /etc/nginx/conf.d/default.conf
10-listen-on-ipv6-by-default.sh: info: Enabled listen on IPv6 in /etc/nginx/conf.d/default.conf
/docker-entrypoint.sh: Launching /docker-entrypoint.d/20-envsubst-on-templates.sh
/docker-entrypoint.sh: Launching /docker-entrypoint.d/30-tune-worker-processes.sh
/docker-entrypoint.sh: Configuration complete; ready for start up
2025/09/11 11:08:09 [notice] 1#1: using the "epoll" event method
2025/09/11 11:08:09 [notice] 1#1: nginx/1.21.6
2025/09/11 11:08:09 [notice] 1#1: built by gcc 10.2.1 20210110 (Debian 10.2.1-6)
2025/09/11 11:08:09 [notice] 1#1: OS: Linux 6.8.0-79-generic
2025/09/11 11:08:09 [notice] 1#1: getrlimit(RLIMIT_NOFILE): 1048576:1048576
2025/09/11 11:08:09 [notice] 1#1: start worker processes
2025/09/11 11:08:09 [notice] 1#1: start worker process 31
2025/09/11 11:08:09 [notice] 1#1: start worker process 32
2025/09/11 11:08:09 [notice] 1#1: start worker process 33
2025/09/11 11:08:09 [notice] 1#1: start worker process 34
```

Figure 7-3. *Output of the kubectl logs command showing application logs from a pod*

For pods containing multiple containers, we need to specify the container name:

```
sudo kubectl logs web-server-pod -c nginx-container
```

```
brando@ubuntu:~$ kubectl logs web-server-pod -c nginx-container
/docker-entrypoint.sh: /docker-entrypoint.d/ is not empty, will attempt to perform configuration
/docker-entrypoint.sh: Looking for shell scripts in /docker-entrypoint.d/
/docker-entrypoint.sh: Launching /docker-entrypoint.d/10-listen-on-ipv6-by-default.sh
10-listen-on-ipv6-by-default.sh: info: Getting the checksum of /etc/nginx/conf.d/default.conf
10-listen-on-ipv6-by-default.sh: info: Enabled listen on IPv6 in /etc/nginx/conf.d/default.conf
/docker-entrypoint.sh: Launching /docker-entrypoint.d/20-envsubst-on-templates.sh
/docker-entrypoint.sh: Launching /docker-entrypoint.d/30-tune-worker-processes.sh
/docker-entrypoint.sh: Configuration complete; ready for start up
2025/09/11 11:08:09 [notice] 1#1: using the "epoll" event method
2025/09/11 11:08:09 [notice] 1#1: nginx/1.21.6
2025/09/11 11:08:09 [notice] 1#1: built by gcc 10.2.1 20210110 (Debian 10.2.1-6)
2025/09/11 11:08:09 [notice] 1#1: OS: Linux 6.8.0-79-generic
2025/09/11 11:08:09 [notice] 1#1: getrlimit(RLIMIT_NOFILE): 1048576:1048576
2025/09/11 11:08:09 [notice] 1#1: start worker processes
2025/09/11 11:08:09 [notice] 1#1: start worker process 31
2025/09/11 11:08:09 [notice] 1#1: start worker process 32
2025/09/11 11:08:09 [notice] 1#1: start worker process 33
2025/09/11 11:08:09 [notice] 1#1: start worker process 34
brando@ubuntu:~$ 
```

Figure 7-4. *Output of kubectl logs command with container name specification for multi-container pods*

We can also get interactive access for real-time troubleshooting within running containers:

```
sudo kubectl exec -it web-server-pod -- /bin/bash
```

This capability allows us to examine file systems, test network connectivity, and run diagnostic commands directly within the pod's execution environment. To exit the interactive session, type exit or press Ctrl+D.

Health Monitoring and Lifecycle Management

Now let's explore how Kubernetes provides sophisticated health monitoring through liveness and readiness probes, extending the self-healing concepts we've discussed throughout previous chapters. Liveness probes determine when containers should be restarted, preventing situations where applications appear to be running but cannot process requests effectively.

Here's an example of a comprehensive health check configuration we can add to our pod specification:

```
monitored-web-pod.yaml
```

```yaml
apiVersion: v1
kind: Pod
metadata:
  name: monitored-web-pod
spec:
  containers:
  - name: nginx
    image: nginx:1.21
    ports:
    - containerPort: 80
    resources:
      requests:
        memory: "128Mi"
        cpu: "250m"
      limits:
        memory: "256Mi"
        cpu: "500m"
    livenessProbe:
      httpGet:
        path: /
        port: 80
      initialDelaySeconds: 30
      periodSeconds: 10
      timeoutSeconds: 5
      failureThreshold: 3
    readinessProbe:
      httpGet:
        path: /
        port: 80
      initialDelaySeconds: 5
      periodSeconds: 5
      timeoutSeconds: 3
      successThreshold: 1
      failureThreshold: 3
```

Let's understand the difference: liveness probes restart containers when they become unresponsive, while readiness probes control traffic flow by removing unhealthy pods from service endpoints. The distinction becomes important when we explore Services and load balancing in later chapters.

We need to carefully tune the probe configuration based on application characteristics. The initialDelaySeconds parameter accounts for startup time, preventing premature failures during initialization. The periodSeconds setting balances responsiveness with resource consumption, while failureThreshold provides tolerance for temporary issues without triggering unnecessary corrective actions.

Resource Management and Node Scheduling

Now we'll examine how resource management directly impacts both pod scheduling and cluster efficiency, building on the architectural concepts from Chapter 4. Resource requests specify minimum requirements that the scheduler uses for placement decisions, while limits define maximum consumption boundaries that prevent resource monopolization.

The kube-scheduler component we discussed in Chapter 5 considers resource requests alongside node capacity, taints, tolerations, and affinity rules when making placement decisions. This complex evaluation ensures optimal resource utilization while respecting scheduling constraints.

Here's how we can define resources in our YAML:

```yaml
resources:
  requests:
    memory: "128Mi"
    cpu: "250m"
  limits:
    memory: "256Mi"
    cpu: "500m"
```

Let's understand resource behavior to help predict application performance under different conditions. Memory limit violations result in pod termination with OutOfMemory errors, while CPU limits cause throttling that reduces performance without terminating containers.

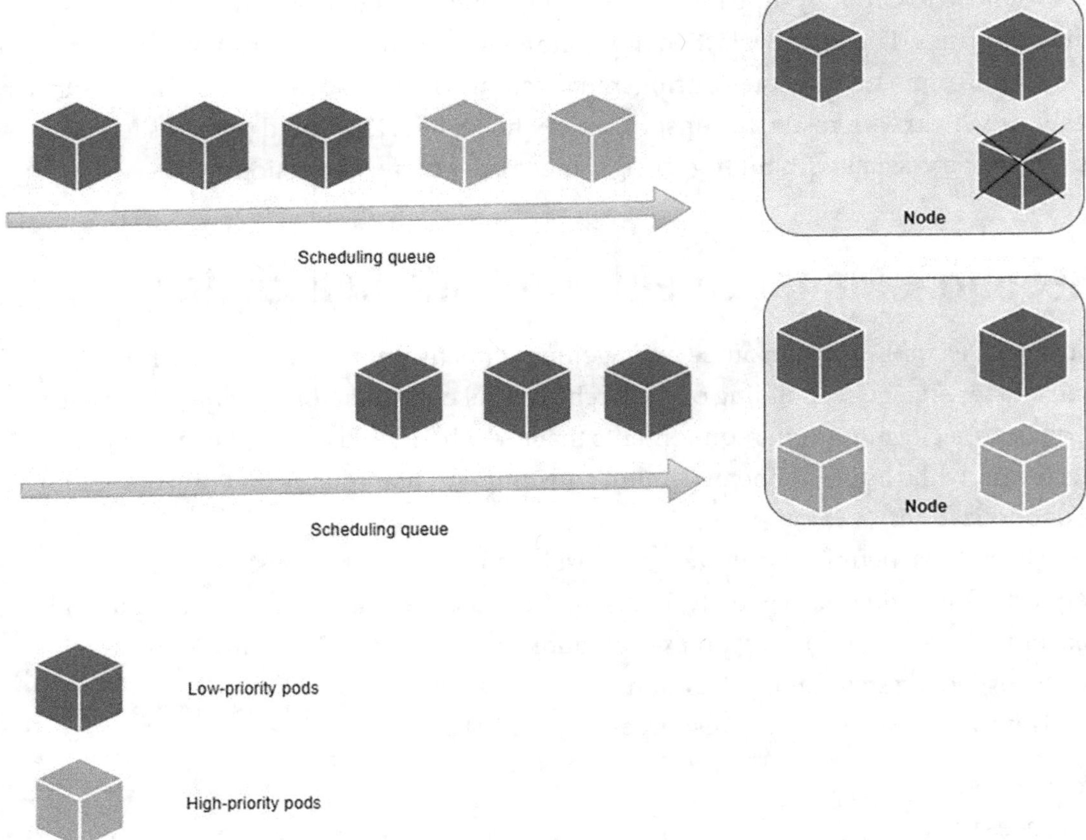

Figure 7-5. *Diagram of Kubernetes scheduler managing pod placement queues with priority-based scheduling*

Figure 7-5 shows the Kubernetes scheduler managing pod placement queues with priority-based scheduling. Higher-priority pods (green) are scheduled ahead of lower-priority pods (blue) in the scheduling queue, demonstrating how the scheduler optimizes resource allocation across available nodes.

Kubernetes encodes pod importance using dedicated PriorityClass resources, each of which defines a numeric value that represents how urgent a workload is for scheduling. Pods opt into these levels by setting the priorityClassName field in their spec, enabling the scheduler to order the queue, favor critical workloads, and decide when lower-priority pods can be preempted to free capacity.

Node selection provides additional control over pod placement through selectors and affinity rules. Simple node selectors use labels to constrain scheduling:

```
spec:
  nodeSelector:
    disk-type: ssd
    environment: production
```

Troubleshooting Common Pod Issues

Let's explore systematic troubleshooting approaches that help resolve pod problems efficiently while minimizing service disruption. We'll cover the most common issues we'll encounter.

When pods remain in Pending status, investigation typically reveals resource constraints, scheduling conflicts, or image availability issues. To see this in practice, we can deliberately create a pod with requirements that no node can satisfy, such as requesting more CPU or memory than any node provides or using a nodeSelector that matches no labels in the cluster. For example, a pod that asks for 2 TB of memory or targets a non-existent label like environment: ultra-production will stay in Pending, allowing us to inspect the scheduling events and understand how the scheduler reports unschedulable workloads. We can check pod events for scheduling problems:

```
sudo kubectl apply -f unschedulable-pod.yaml
sudo kubectl get pod unschedulable-pod
```

We can then check pod events for scheduling problems:

```
sudo kubectl describe pod unschedulable-pod
```

Look for messages about insufficient resources, node selector mismatches, or taint/toleration conflicts in the Events section.

CrashLoopBackOff indicates pods are starting but failing repeatedly. The exponential backoff mechanism increases the delay between restart attempts, preventing resource exhaustion while the underlying issue persists. To experiment with this state, we can deploy a pod that always exits with an error, such as a container that runs a simple script and returns a non-zero status code on startup. After a few restart attempts, the pod will enter CrashLoopBackOff, giving us a safe way to observe how Kubernetes reports repeated failures and applies exponential backoff. We can examine logs from failed containers:

```
sudo kubectl logs failing-pod --previous
```

Application configuration errors, missing dependencies, or environmental issues typically cause these restart loops.

For network connectivity problems, we need a methodical investigation. Let's test basic connectivity from within pods:

```
sudo kubectl exec -it network-test-pod -- ping google.com
```

```
sudo kubectl exec -it network-test-pod -- nslookup kubernetes.default
```

These tests help us isolate whether issues stem from network configuration, DNS resolution, or application-specific problems.

Storage-related issues may prevent pods from accessing required volumes or configuration data. We can verify volume mounts and persistent volume claims:

In some cases, pods fail because they cannot read the data or configuration they need from storage, such as when a container expects files that are missing or inaccessible inside its filesystem. At this stage, it is enough to recognize that storage misconfiguration can cause pods to crash or stay in Pending, and we will explore how Kubernetes volumes and persistent storage work in a later chapter.

Production Best Practices

Let's discuss production pod management, which requires disciplined approaches that promote reliability and operational efficiency. We should always define resource requests and limits based on application profiling and monitoring data. Start with conservative estimates and adjust based on observed behavior rather than guessing resource requirements.

We need to implement comprehensive health checks using both liveness and readiness probes with appropriate timeout values and failure thresholds. Avoid overly aggressive settings that cause unnecessary restarts while ensuring prompt detection of genuine problems.

Let's use consistent labeling strategies that support operational activities and automation. Include information about application versions, environments, teams, and business purposes:

metadata:

```
labels:
  app: web-server
  version: v1.21.3
  environment: production
  team: platform
  component: frontend
```

We should also plan for graceful shutdowns using preStop hooks and appropriate termination grace periods. This preparation becomes particularly important for stateful applications or those handling long-running transactions.

Integration with Controller Patterns

While understanding direct pod management remains essential, production environments typically rely on higher-level controllers. Let's understand how these work together.

Deployments provide rolling updates and self-healing through ReplicaSets, making them suitable for stateless applications. StatefulSets offer ordered deployment and stable identities for stateful workloads, while DaemonSets ensure specific pods run on designated nodes. Understanding the relationship between pods and their managing controllers enables more effective troubleshooting and operational procedures. When issues occur, investigating controller status often provides insights that aren't apparent from examining pods in isolation. The skills we've developed in pod management provide the foundation for working with these higher-level abstractions while maintaining the ability to troubleshoot at the fundamental level when necessary. This combination of direct pod knowledge with controller understanding creates the operational expertise needed for successful Kubernetes deployments at scale.

Now that we've mastered pod management, we're ready to explore how Deployments and ReplicaSets build upon these concepts in the next chapter. These higher-level controllers will help us manage pods more effectively in production environments while maintaining the reliability and self-healing properties we've learned about here.

Summary

We defined pods as Kubernetes' approach to grouping containers that work closely together, creating a shared execution environment where containers communicate through localhost. We also explored how pods are ephemeral by design, meaning Kubernetes replaces failed pods rather than attempting repairs. We examined the five pod lifecycle phases, Pending, Running, Succeeded, Failed, and Unknown, that provide visibility into deployment status. And at the end, we reviewed the essential kubectl commands: get pods for status visibility, describe for comprehensive configuration and event details, and logs for direct application insight.

In the next chapter, we will explore how Kubernetes automates pod management at scale through Deployments, which manage pods via ReplicaSets for stateless workloads while maintaining the pod management principles we have just mastered.

CHAPTER 8

Deployments and ReplicaSets

Introduction

Welcome to application orchestration. By now, we have successfully created and run individual Pods, which is a massive first step. However, we might be wondering: what happens if one of those Pods crashes while we are asleep? Or what if our application suddenly becomes popular and a single Pod can no longer handle the traffic?

In this chapter, we will solve these problems by introducing the "managers" of the Kubernetes world: ReplicaSets and Deployments. We will move away from manually creating fragile, standalone Pods and start building resilient systems that can heal themselves and scale on demand. We will explore how Kubernetes ensures our application matches the state we desire, automatically handling failures so we don't have to.

Objectives

By the end of this chapter, we will be able to

- Understand why managing individual Pods is insufficient for production environments

- Explain how ReplicaSets provide self-healing capabilities by maintaining a stable number of Pods

- Master the hierarchical relationship between Deployments, ReplicaSets, and Pods

© Brando Marzio Sabatini 2026
B. M. Sabatini, *Kubernetes for Absolute Beginners*, https://doi.org/10.1007/979-8-8688-2445-6_8

- Scale applications up and down effectively to meet changing demand

- Deploy robust applications that can survive node failures and unexpected crashes

Managing individual Pods directly in production environments becomes increasingly complex as applications scale. While we can create and run Pods using the kubectl run command, this approach lacks the resilience and automation that modern containerized applications require. When a Pod crashes, gets deleted, or fails unexpectedly, there's no mechanism to automatically restore it. This limitation leads us to explore more sophisticated Kubernetes objects designed to ensure our applications remain available and can scale according to demand.

Understanding ReplicaSets

ReplicaSets maintain a stable set of identical Pod replicas by enforcing a specified count. The ReplicaSet controller continuously monitors running Pods and automatically creates or terminates instances to match our desired state. If a pod crashes or gets deleted, the ReplicaSet starts a new one to replace it, provided cluster resources allow it (e.g., no node failures or quota issues prevent recreation). It also removes extra pods, so the number of the running replicas matches the "spec.replicas" field of the YAML configuration file.

Conceptually, a ReplicaSet functions as a control loop: it continuously observes our cluster's Pod population, compares it against the desired state we have declared, and takes corrective action. Unlike systems that track individual object identities, ReplicaSets use label-based selectors, meaning they manage any Pod matching our label criteria, not specific named instances. The ReplicaSet doesn't care about individual Pod identities— it only ensures the correct number of Pods matching its selector are running. When Pods are created or recreated, they receive new names and potentially new IP addresses, making ReplicaSets ideal for stateless applications.

ReplicaSets use label selectors to determine which Pods they should manage. They match labels on Pods and only manage those that fit the criteria. The ReplicaSet doesn't track individual Pods by name, but by this set of labels, ensuring the desired number of matching Pods are always operational.

Below is an example YAML file for a ReplicaSet named nginx-replicaset, which maintains three replicas of an NGINX Pod, each running nginx:1.25 on port 80:

nginx-replicaset.yaml

```
apiVersion: apps/v1
kind: ReplicaSet
metadata:
  name: nginx-replicaset
  labels:
    app: nginx
spec:
  replicas: 3
  selector:
    matchLabels:
      app: nginx
  template:
    metadata:
      labels:
        app: nginx
    spec:
      containers:
        - name: nginx
          image: nginx:1.25
          ports:
            - containerPort: 80
```

We can create this ReplicaSet with:

(Copy and paste the previous text inside the YAML file, then write and save the nano editor.)

nano nginx-replicaset.yaml
sudo kubectl apply -f nginx-replicaset.yaml

After creating this ReplicaSet, we can check its status using the command:

sudo kubectl get rs

To get more details about a ReplicaSet, we use this command:

```
sudo kubectl describe rs nginx-replicaset
```

Understanding Why Pod Names Differ

When we create a ReplicaSet that manages existing Pods, we may notice that newly created Pods have different names than expected. This occurs because the ReplicaSet controller uses the label selector to identify which Pods it should manage. If a Pod already exists with the matching label (for example, app=nginx) from a previous deployment or manual creation, the ReplicaSet recognizes it as a managed Pod and counts it toward the desired replica count.

For instance, if we previously created a Pod named nginx-manual with the label app=nginx and then create a ReplicaSet with spec.replicas: 3 using the same label selector, the ReplicaSet will only create two additional Pods instead of three. The existing Pod is now under ReplicaSet management. The newly created Pods will receive names following the pattern nginx-replicaset-xxxxx (where xxxxx is a random suffix), while the manually created Pod retains its original name. This behavior demonstrates that ReplicaSets manage Pods by label selector rather than by individual naming conventions.

Testing ReplicaSet Self-Healing

We can verify that our ReplicaSet is working properly by listing the pods it manages:

```
sudo kubectl get pods
```

If we manually delete one of the managed Pods (e.g., sudo kubectl delete pod nginx-replicaset-abc12), the ReplicaSet will notice and create a replacement Pod, demonstrating its self-healing property.

```
sudo kubectl delete pod nginx-replicaset-abc12
sudo kubectl get pods
```

Within seconds, we'll see a new Pod created to maintain the desired replica count.

Scaling Up and Down

One of the primary functions of a ReplicaSet is the ability to scale our application by adjusting the replica count. We can modify the number of replicas by editing the ReplicaSet:

```
sudo kubectl edit rs nginx-replicaset
```

This opens the YAML definition in our default editor. Locate the spec.replicas field and change it from 3 to 5, then save and exit. The ReplicaSet controller will immediately work to create two additional Pods to match the new desired state.

```
sudo kubectl get rs
sudo kubectl get pods
```

Similarly, we can scale down by reducing the spec.replicas value:

```
sudo kubectl edit rs nginx-replicaset
```

Change spec.replicas from 5 to 2. The ReplicaSet will terminate three Pods to match the new desired state:

```
sudo kubectl get rs
sudo kubectl get pods
```

Understanding Resource Constraints

It's important to recognize that a ReplicaSet can only maintain its desired number of replicas if sufficient cluster resources are available. If our cluster runs out of resources—such as available CPU, memory, or disk space on the worker nodes—the ReplicaSet cannot create new Pods to replace failed ones or to scale up. When attempting to create a Pod and insufficient resources are available, the Pod will remain in a Pending state indefinitely.

We can observe this condition by examining the ReplicaSet and Pod status:

```
sudo kubectl describe rs nginx-replicaset
sudo kubectl describe pod nginx-replicaset-abc12
```

The Events section will indicate resource constraint messages such as Insufficient memory or Insufficient cpu. This is why resource planning and monitoring are critical aspects of Kubernetes cluster management.

The Relationship Between Deployments and ReplicaSets

While ReplicaSets provide essential Pod management capabilities, Deployments offer a more comprehensive solution for application lifecycle management. ReplicaSets are not usually created directly; they are created through the deployments object.

The relationship works like this: Deployments manage ReplicaSets, ReplicaSets manage Pods, and Pods run containers. This hierarchical structure enables sophisticated update strategies while maintaining the underlying reliability of ReplicaSet-managed Pods.

Below is an example YAML file for a Deployment named nginx-deployment, which manages three replicas of the same NGINX Pod:

`nginx-dep.yaml`

```yaml
apiVersion: apps/v1
kind: Deployment
metadata:
  name: nginx-deployment
  labels:
    app: nginx
spec:
  replicas: 3
  selector:
    matchLabels:
      app: nginx
  template:
    metadata:
      labels:
        app: nginx
    spec:
      containers:
        - name: nginx
          image: nginx:1.25
          ports:
            - containerPort: 80
```

Deployments are controlled by the deployment controller manager, and the ReplicaSets are controlled by the ReplicaSet controller manager. When we create a deployment using the following command:

(Copy and paste the previous text inside the YAML file, then write and save the nano editor.)

```
nano nginx-dep.yaml
sudo kubectl apply -f nginx-dep.yaml
```

We can check the details of our deployment after it is created using

```
sudo kubectl get deployments
sudo kubectl describe deployment nginx-deployment
```

The output will show us that the "nginx-dep" deployment is running three pod replicas.

We can also see the newly created ReplicaSet and associated Pods using the previous kubectl get replicaset and kubectl get pods commands.

Scaling Applications with HPA Integration

One of the key advantages of using Deployments and ReplicaSets is their integration with Kubernetes' scaling mechanisms. The hierarchical structure we've established provides the foundation for both manual and automatic scaling of our applications.

Manual Scaling

We can manually scale a Deployment by modifying the replica count, just as with ReplicaSets:

```
sudo kubectl scale deployment nginx-deployment --replicas=5
```

This command immediately updates the Deployment, and the underlying ReplicaSet will work to create additional Pods. Let's verify the scaling operation:

```
sudo kubectl get deployment nginx-deployment
sudo kubectl get pods -l app=nginx
```

Horizontal Pod Autoscaler (HPA)

For more sophisticated scaling scenarios, Kubernetes provides the Horizontal Pod Autoscaler (HPA), which automatically adjusts the number of replicas based on observed metrics such as CPU utilization or memory usage. The HPA monitors our Deployment and dynamically scales the replica count to maintain our specified target metrics.

First, ensure that our cluster has metrics enabled (typically requires the metrics-server to be installed):

```
sudo kubectl get deployment metrics-server -n kube-system
```

Create an HPA resource for our nginx-deployment:

Note   Containers require .spec.containers[].resources.requests.cpu to be set.

---

nginx-hpa.yaml

```
apiVersion: autoscaling/v2
kind: HorizontalPodAutoscaler
metadata:
  name: nginx-hpa
spec:
  scaleTargetRef:
    apiVersion: apps/v1
    kind: Deployment
    name: nginx-deployment
  minReplicas: 2
  maxReplicas: 10
  metrics:
  - type: Resource
    resource:
      name: cpu
      target:
        type: Utilization
        averageUtilization: 70
```

Apply the HPA configuration:

```
nano nginx-hpa.yaml
sudo kubectl apply -f nginx-hpa.yaml
```

Monitor the HPA status:

```
sudo kubectl get hpa
sudo kubectl describe hpa nginx-hpa
```

When CPU utilization exceeds our target threshold (70% in this example), the HPA automatically increases the replica count up to the maxReplicas limit. However, HPA includes a 10% tolerance threshold to prevent constant scaling fluctuations. When our target is 70%, it will scale up at 80% utilization and scale down at 60% utilization. Conversely, when utilization drops below the threshold, it gradually scales down to the minReplicas value. This ensures our application maintains performance during traffic spikes while optimizing resource utilization during low-demand periods.

The HPA works seamlessly with both ReplicaSets and Deployments, automatically managing the spec.replicas field based on real-time metrics. This makes it an essential tool for production environments where demand varies unpredictably.

Summary

In this chapter, we made the crucial transition from running simple containers to managing resilient applications. We explored how ReplicaSets act as a safety net, continuously monitoring the cluster to ensure that if a Pod fails, a new one immediately takes its place. We also learned that while ReplicaSets handle the heavy lifting of reliability, Deployments are the higher-level tool we use to manage the lifecycle and updates of our software.

We now have applications that are both self-healing and scalable—two pillars of modern infrastructure. However, having running applications is only half the battle. As these Pods scale up and move around the cluster, their IP addresses change. How do we ensure they can consistently find and talk to each other?

In the next chapter, we will dive into Kubernetes Networking to unravel the mysteries of communication and service discovery.

CHAPTER 9

Kubernetes Networking

Introduction

Welcome to Kubernetes networking. By now, we have created pods, deployed applications with services, and watched them scale across our cluster. But we might be wondering: how do these pods actually talk to each other? How does a request from outside the cluster reach the right pod? And how do we keep traffic secure?

In this chapter, we will answer these questions by exploring how Kubernetes networking actually works. We will start with the basics: how pods get IP addresses and can communicate directly. Then we will look at services and the different ways to expose our applications. We will explore network policies that act like firewall rules to protect our applications. Then, we will see how to troubleshoot networking problems when things don't work as expected.

By the end of this chapter, we will understand how all the networking pieces fit together, and we will be able to configure and troubleshoot networking for our own Kubernetes applications.

Objectives

By the end of this chapter, we will be able to

- Understand how pods receive IP addresses and communicate with each other

- Know how service discovery and DNS work in Kubernetes clusters

- Create and use the three main service types: ClusterIP, NodePort, and LoadBalancer

© Brando Marzio Sabatini 2026

B. M. Sabatini, *Kubernetes for Absolute Beginners*, https://doi.org/10.1007/979-8-8688-2445-6_9

- Use network policies to control which pods can communicate with each other

- Configure Ingress to route HTTP and HTTPS traffic to our services

- Troubleshoot networking problems using kubectl commands

Building upon our understanding of pods, services, and deployments from previous chapters, we now explore networking in Kubernetes. As our applications grow from simple single-pod demonstrations to multiservice production systems, understanding how these components communicate becomes essential. Kubernetes networking provides the foundation that enables our pods to discover each other, services to route traffic efficiently, and external users to access our applications securely.

Think of Kubernetes networking as the postal system for our cluster. Just as the postal service ensures letters reach their intended recipients regardless of where they move, Kubernetes networking ensures that requests find their way to the correct pods, even as they are created, destroyed, and replaced throughout the cluster lifecycle. This chapter builds directly on the concepts we established with pods, services, and YAML configurations, showing us how these pieces work together to create a cohesive communication infrastructure.

How Pod Networking Works

When we created our first pods in earlier chapters, each pod automatically received its own IP address. This fundamental networking principle ensures that every pod can communicate with every other pod in the cluster without complex configuration. Behind this apparent simplicity lies the Container Network Interface (CNI), which handles the technical details of assigning IP addresses and establishing network connectivity.

The CNI acts as the networking foundation for our entire cluster. When the kubelet creates a new pod, it calls the CNI plugin to configure networking for that pod's containers. The CNI plugin assigns an IP address from the cluster's network range, creates the necessary network interfaces, and establishes routing rules that enable communication with other pods and services.

Different CNI plugins provide various networking approaches optimized for specific needs. Flannel offers straightforward overlay networking that works reliably across different environments. Calico provides more sophisticated routing with enhanced security policy capabilities. For K3s installations, like we demonstrated in Chapter 3,

Flannel typically serves as the default CNI, providing simple and effective networking for learning and development scenarios.

We can observe our cluster's networking configuration by examining the network interfaces and routing tables on our nodes. Each pod receives its IP address from a subnet allocated to the node where it runs, ensuring that IP addresses remain unique across the entire cluster.

Service Discovery and DNS

Services rely on the labels and selectors we introduced in previous chapters to identify their target pods. Once the connection is established via these selectors, applications need a way to discover and connect to these services.

When we create a service using the YAML configurations we practiced in earlier chapters, Kubernetes immediately registers that service in the cluster's DNS system. Applications can then connect to services using predictable DNS names instead of IP addresses, which may change as pods are recreated.

For a service, we define a named web service in the default namespace; pods can connect using the full name web-service.default.svc.cluster.local or simply web-service when connecting from within the same namespace.

Figure 9-1 shows the fundamental traffic flow in Kubernetes, showing how external requests reach a Service component, which then uses kube-proxy to distribute traffic across multiple backend Pods. The kube-proxy component acts as the network proxy on each node, maintaining the network rules that enable service abstraction and load balancing to the underlying pod endpoints.

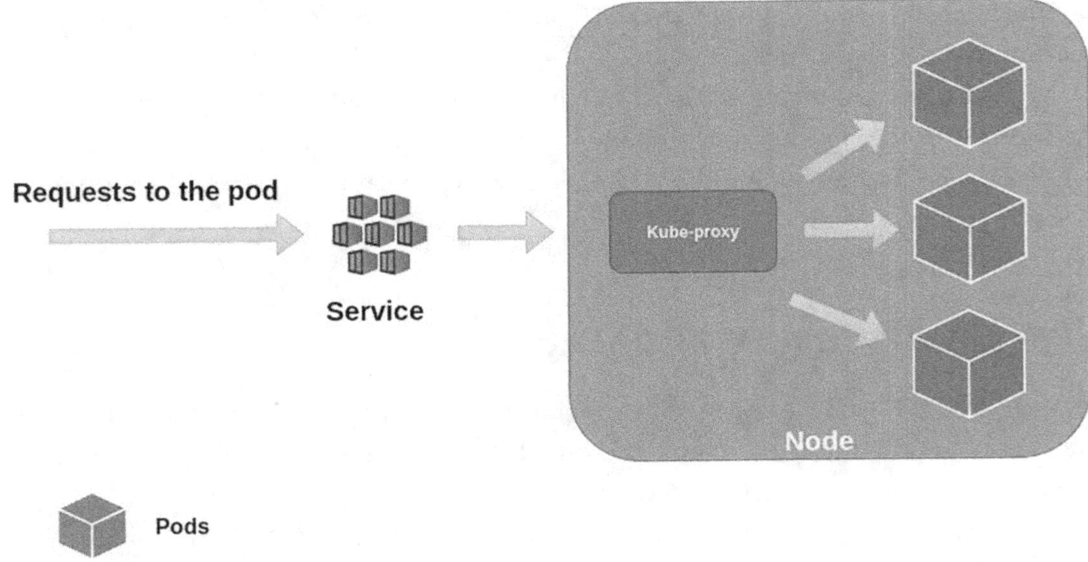

Figure 9-1. *Kube-proxy load balances service traffic*

Understanding Service Types

The services we've created so far used the ClusterIP type, which makes services accessible only within the cluster. Kubernetes provides several service types that determine how and where our applications can be accessed. These service types form a hierarchical relationship; each type builds upon the previous one, adding capabilities while maintaining the functionality of its predecessor.

ClusterIP services provide internal connectivity within the cluster. These services receive virtual IP addresses that exist only within the cluster network, making them perfect for communication between different components of our application. The ReplicaSets and Deployments we created in Chapter 8 typically connect to databases, caching layers, and other internal services through ClusterIP services.

Let's create a ClusterIP to use:

```
nano web-service.yaml
```

```
web-service.yaml
```

```yaml
apiVersion: v1
kind: Service
metadata:
  name: web-service
spec:
  type: ClusterIP
  selector:
    app: web
  ports:
  - protocol: TCP
    port: 80
    targetPort: 80
```

Apply this service:

```
sudo kubectl apply -f web-service.yaml
```

NodePort Services extend ClusterIP functionality by also exposing the service on a specific port on every node in the cluster. When we create a NodePort service, Kubernetes automatically allocates a port in the range 30000–32767 on each node and forwards traffic from that port to our service. Importantly, the NodePort service maintains the ClusterIP functionality as well—internal pods can still connect using the service name while external clients can access via the node port.

Let's create a NodePort service that builds on our internal ClusterIP service:

```
nano web-nodeport-service.yaml
```

```
web-nodeport-service.yaml
```

```yaml
apiVersion: v1
kind: Service
metadata:
  name: web-nodeport-service
spec:
  type: NodePort
  selector:
    app: web
  ports:
  - protocol: TCP
    port: 80
    targetPort: 80
    nodePort: 30080
```

Let's apply this service:

```
sudo kubectl apply -f web-nodeport-service.yaml
```

Now we can access our application from outside the cluster using any node's IP address and port 30080, while internal services continue to use the ClusterIP. This service type proves particularly useful for development environments and situations where we need external access without cloud provider load balancers.

LoadBalancer Services represent the most comprehensive external access method. When we create a LoadBalancer service in a cloud environment, Kubernetes coordinates with our cloud provider to provision an actual load balancer that distributes traffic across our cluster nodes. Like NodePort, the LoadBalancer maintains both ClusterIP and NodePort functionality, adding an external entry point. This integration provides professional-grade external access with health checks, SSL termination, and automatic failover capabilities.

Network Policies for Security

Just as ConfigMaps and Secrets help secure application configuration, Network Policies provide security controls for network traffic. By default, Kubernetes allows unrestricted communication between pods, which creates potential security risks as our applications grow more complex.

Network Policies function like firewall rules, allowing us to specify which pods can communicate with each other and on which ports. They use the same label selectors we explored in Chapter 11 to identify source and destination pods, providing fine-grained control over network traffic.

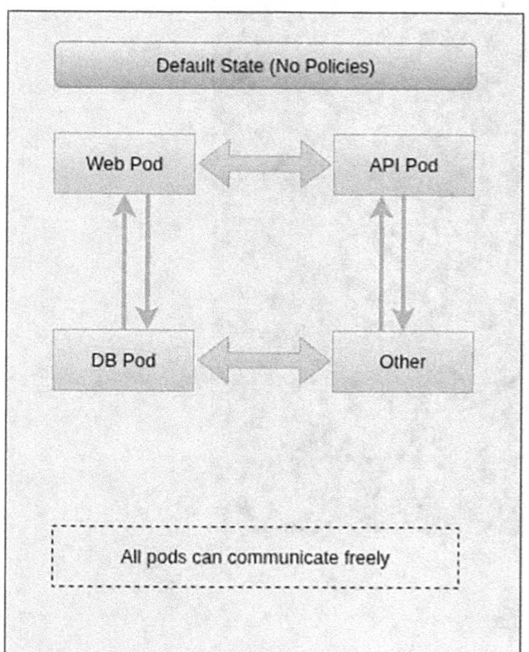

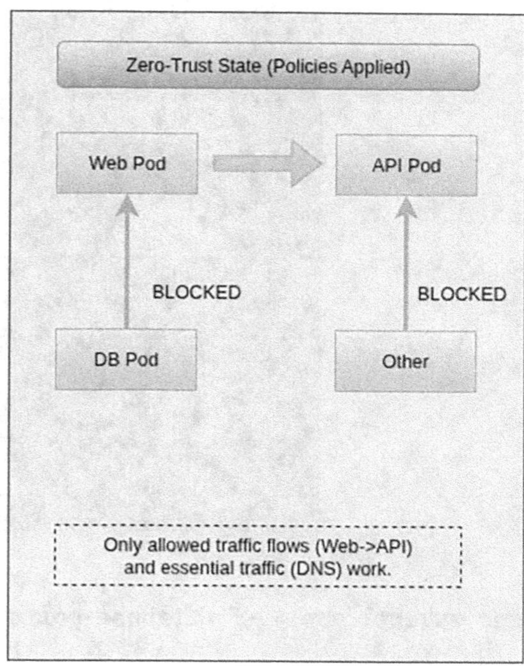

Figure 9-2. *Default vs. zero-trust network policies*

This diagram shows how Kubernetes Network Policies create a zero-trust security model. In the "Default State," all pods within a namespace can communicate freely. After applying a "Default Deny" policy and specific "Allow" policies, only explicitly permitted traffic flows are possible, blocking all other communication and enhancing security (see Figure 9-2).

Here's a basic network policy that demonstrates how to restrict access to a database service:

nano database-policy.yaml

database-policy.yaml

```yaml
apiVersion: networking.k8s.io/v1
kind: NetworkPolicy
metadata:
  name: database-policy
spec:
  podSelector:
    matchLabels:
      app: database
  policyTypes:
    - Ingress
  ingress:
    - from:
        - podSelector:
            matchLabels:
              app: web
      ports:
        - protocol: TCP
          port: 3306
```

```
sudo kubectl apply -f database-policy.yaml
```

This policy ensures that only pods labeled app: web can connect to pods labeled app: database on port 3306. All other traffic to the database pods is blocked, significantly improving security.

Network Policies require a CNI plugin that supports policy enforcement. While basic plugins like Flannel focus on connectivity, policy-capable plugins like Calico or Cilium can enforce these security rules at the network level.

Ingress Controllers and External Access

While NodePort and LoadBalancer services provide external access, Ingress offers a more sophisticated approach for HTTP and HTTPS traffic. Ingress operates at the application layer, enabling features like path-based routing, SSL termination, and virtual hosting that aren't available with basic service types.

An Ingress resource defines rules for routing external HTTP traffic to services within our cluster. However, Ingress resources don't work by themselves—they require an Ingress Controller to implement the actual traffic routing. Popular Ingress Controllers include NGINX Ingress Controller, Traefik, and cloud provider-specific solutions.

For K3s installations, Traefik comes preinstalled as the default Ingress Controller, making it easy to experiment with Ingress concepts. Here's an example Ingress configuration that routes traffic based on paths:

nano web-ingress.yaml

web-ingress.yaml

```
apiVersion: networking.k8s.io/v1
kind: Ingress
metadata:
  name: web-ingress
spec:
  rules:
    - host: web.local
      http:
        paths:
          - path: /
            pathType: Prefix
            backend:
              service:
                name: web-service
                port:
                  number: 80
```

sudo kubectl apply -f web-ingress.yaml

This Ingress configuration routes HTTP requests for web.local to our web service. We can add multiple rules to handle different hostnames or paths, enabling sophisticated routing scenarios with a single external IP address.

Configuring Local DNS Resolution

Since web.local is not a public domain name, our server needs a local mapping to resolve it correctly. We must modify the hosts file to direct traffic for this domain to our local cluster.

Open the hosts file for editing:

```
sudo nano /etc/hosts
```

Add this line to the bottom of the file to map the domain to our localhost:

```
127.0.0.1 web.local
```

Save and exit. We can now test the Ingress configuration directly from the command line using curl:

```
curl http://web.local
```

Troubleshooting Network Connectivity

Important   Before troubleshooting, ensure our web service is active by running sudo kubectl get services. If the service is missing, the following tests will fail.

Understanding how to diagnose networking issues helps maintain reliable applications. Kubernetes provides several tools and techniques for troubleshooting connectivity problems.

Start with basic connectivity tests using temporary pods:

(Use this to test from a pod, where DNS works.)

```
kubectl run -it --rm debug --image=busybox --restart=Never -- wget -qO-
http://web-service
```

From within this pod, we can test DNS resolution:

```
nslookup web-service
```

Test HTTP connectivity:

```
wget -qO- http://web-service
```

Check network policies and service endpoints:

sudo kubectl get networkpolicies

View service endpoints:

sudo kubectl get endpoints

As shown in Figure 9-4, we can describe a service:

sudo kubectl describe service web-service

Examine service and pod logs shown in Figure 9-3:

kubectl logs deployment/web-app

or

kubectl logs -l app=web

Figure 9-3. *Kubernetes web app deployment startup logs*

```
sudo kubectl describe service web-service
```

```
brando@ubuntu:~$ kubectl describe service web-service
Name:                   web-service
Namespace:              default
Labels:                 <none>
Annotations:            <none>
Selector:               app=web
Type:                   ClusterIP
IP Family Policy:       SingleStack
IP Families:            IPv4
IP:                     10.43.249.216
IPs:                    10.43.249.216
Port:                   <unset>   80/TCP
TargetPort:             80/TCP
Endpoints:              10.42.0.177:80,10.42.0.184:80,10.42.0.182:80 + 2 more...
Session Affinity:       None
Internal Traffic Policy: Cluster
Events:                 <none>
brando@ubuntu:~$ []
```

Figure 9-4. *Kubernetes web service detailed description*

These troubleshooting techniques help identify whether connectivity issues stem from DNS problems, network policies, service configuration, or application-level problems.

Practical Network Architecture

Building upon the deployment patterns we established in Chapter 8, let's examine how networking decisions affect application architecture. A typical multitier application includes frontend services accessible from outside the cluster, backend APIs that handle business logic, and databases that store persistent data.

The frontend tier typically uses LoadBalancer or Ingress for external access, enabling users to reach our application from the internet. The backend tier uses ClusterIP services for internal communication, providing stable endpoints for the frontend to call APIs and business logic services. The database tier also uses ClusterIP services but with restrictive Network Policies that allow connections only from authorized backend services.

This architecture leverages the hierarchical nature of Kubernetes networking, where each layer provides appropriate access controls and connectivity options. External users access only the frontend components, frontend components connect to backend APIs through internal services, and backend components connect to databases through tightly controlled service endpoints.

The service discovery mechanisms we explored ensure that these connections remain functional even as pods are recreated, scaled, or moved between nodes. The YAML configurations we practiced in Chapter 6 define these networking relationships declaratively, making the entire architecture reproducible and maintainable.

Understanding Kubernetes networking prepares us to build applications that can scale reliably, communicate securely, and adapt to changing infrastructure requirements. These networking concepts integrate directly with the pod lifecycle management, service abstractions, and configuration patterns we've established in previous chapters, providing the foundation for production-ready Kubernetes deployments.

Summary

In this chapter, we learned how Kubernetes networking enables pods and services to communicate. We started by understanding how each pod automatically gets its own IP address through the Container Network Interface (CNI) and how this allows pods to communicate directly without any complex setup. We then explored how Kubernetes DNS makes it possible for pods to find services by name instead of remembering IP addresses. We examined the three main service types we will use in practice: ClusterIP for communication within our cluster, NodePort for exposing services on specific ports across nodes, and LoadBalancer for using cloud provider load balancers. We learned that these service types build upon each other, with each one adding more external access options while keeping the internal functionality. We also learned how network policies work like firewall rules, allowing us to control which pods can talk to each other and on which ports. We saw how Ingress provides a more sophisticated way to route HTTP and HTTPS traffic based on paths and hostnames. And we covered practical troubleshooting techniques using kubectl commands and showed how all these networking pieces work together in a real application with frontend, backend, and database tiers. These networking concepts connect directly to the pods and services we created in previous chapters, and they form the foundation for building reliable applications in Kubernetes.

In the next chapter, we will explore ConfigMaps and Secrets, which allow us to manage configuration and sensitive data for our applications without rebuilding our container images.

CHAPTER 10

ConfigMaps and Secrets

Introduction

As our Kubernetes deployments expand from simple prototypes into mission-critical services, the challenge of managing configuration and protecting sensitive data becomes increasingly important. Applications need to adapt across different environments—development, staging, production—without requiring code changes or image rebuilds. Kubernetes addresses this with two complementary resources: ConfigMaps for nonsensitive configuration data and Secrets for protecting sensitive information like credentials and encryption keys.

Objectives

By the end of this chapter, we will be able to

- Create and manage ConfigMaps to store nonsensitive configuration data separately from our container images

- Deploy Secrets to securely handle sensitive information such as credentials, API keys, and private keys with encryption and access controls

- Mount ConfigMaps and Secrets as files or inject them as environment variables within our Pods

- Understand the security benefits of mounting Secrets as tmpfs volumes and implement best practices for protecting sensitive data

- Apply configuration updates to running workloads without rebuilding or redeploying container images

© Brando Marzio Sabatini 2026

B. M. Sabatini, *Kubernetes for Absolute Beginners*, https://doi.org/10.1007/979-8-8688-2445-6_10

As our Kubernetes workloads grow from small experiments to critical business services, keeping configuration clean and secret data protected becomes essential. Configuration management lets us adapt applications to different environments—development, testing, or production—without changing our code or rebuilding container images. Kubernetes provides dedicated resources, called ConfigMaps and Secrets, to handle both configuration and sensitive data in a flexible and secure way.

In earlier projects, it might have been tempting to hard-code an API endpoint or a debug flag inside our application. While this works short-term, it becomes unmanageable as environments, requirements, or credentials change. Instead, Kubernetes helps us decouple configuration from code with ConfigMaps and keeps confidential data such as passwords or access tokens secure using Secrets.

A ConfigMap holds nonsensitive key-value pairs like application modes, service URLs, or feature flags outside of our container images. This means the same image can be reused everywhere, with the only difference being the associated ConfigMap for each environment. To define a ConfigMap, we can use a YAML file like the following (which is saved as, for example, app-config.yaml):

app-config.yaml

```
apiVersion: v1
kind: ConfigMap
metadata:
  name: app-config
data:
  LOG_LEVEL: "info"
  FEATURE_X_ENABLED: "true"
  API_URL: "https://api.example.com"
```

Apply this ConfigMap to our cluster with:

(Copy and paste the previous text inside the YAML file, then write and save the nano editor.)

```
nano app-config.yaml
sudo kubectl apply -f app-config.yaml
```

With the ConfigMap created, we can reference these key-value pairs as environment variables inside our Pods or mount them as configuration files that our application will read at runtime. This approach speeds up environment-specific changes and keeps our images and deployments generic and easy to maintain.

While ConfigMaps address plain configuration, any sensitive value, such as a password or a private key, needs the extra protection of a Secret. Kubernetes Secrets are stored as base64 encoded values, can be encrypted at rest, and are tightly regulated with RBAC (role-based access control) rules, reducing the risk of accidental exposure. While ConfigMaps work well for nonsensitive data, mounting them as volumes offers flexibility when applications expect configuration files on the filesystem.

For practical application, mounting ConfigMaps and Secrets as volumes is often preferred. Consider a Deployment that mounts a ConfigMap containing application settings:

app-settings.yaml

```yaml
apiVersion: v1
kind: ConfigMap
metadata:
  name: app-settings
data:
  config.ini: |
    debug=false
    log_level=info
```

app-deployment (first_part).yaml

When the Pod starts, the ConfigMap data becomes available as files at /etc/config/config.ini inside the container. For Secrets, the mounting mechanism is identical, but Kubernetes backs the mount with a tmpfs (ramdisk)—meaning the Secret data exists only in memory and is never written to disk, significantly reducing exposure risk for sensitive information like passwords or private keys.

This method is particularly useful for legacy applications or third-party software that reads configuration from mounted paths. For example, to securely provide a database username and password to our application, we might create a YAML file called db-credentials.yaml:

```
apiVersion: apps/v1
kind: Deployment
metadata:
  name: app-deployment
spec:
  template:
    spec:
      containers:
      - name: app
        image: myapp:latest
        volumeMounts:
        - name: config-volume
          mountPath: /etc/config
      volumes:
      - name: config-volume
        configMap:
          name: app-settings
```

db-credentials.yaml

```
apiVersion: v1
kind: Secret
metadata:
  name: db-credentials
type: Opaque
data:
  username: YWRtaW4=
  password: c3VwZXJzZWNyZXQ=
```

Here, "YWRtaW4=" is the base64 representation of "admin," and "c3VwZXJzZWNyZXQ=" is "supersecret." Secrets are consumed just like ConfigMaps, through environment variables or by mounting them as files accessible within the Pod. Create the secret with:

(Copy and paste the previous text inside the YAML file, then write and save the nano editor.)

```
nano db-credentials.yaml
sudo kubectl apply -f db-credentials.yaml
```

To inject values from ConfigMaps and Secrets directly as environment variables, we update the env section of our Pod specification. While mounting configuration as files (discussed earlier) is generally preferred, especially for larger, more complex, or frequently updated data mapping to environment variables can still be acceptable for small, simple, and immutable settings.

For example, to set our app's log level and securely load database credentials:

```
app-deployment (second_part).yaml
```

```
env:
  - name: LOG_LEVEL
    valueFrom:
      configMapKeyRef:
        name: app-config
        key: LOG_LEVEL
  - name: DB_USER
    valueFrom:
      secretKeyRef:
        name: db-credentials
        key: username
  - name: DB_PASS
    valueFrom:
      secretKeyRef:
        name: db-credentials
        key: password
```

Important   In the following command, <pod-name> should be replaced with the actual pod's name.

Once deployed, we can verify that the values are correctly injected by executing a shell command inside the running Pod to print the environment variables:

```
kubectl exec <pod-name> -- printenv | grep -E 'LOG_LEVEL|DB'
```

With this pattern, changing our configuration or rotating secrets no longer requires building and pushing new images. We simply update the relevant ConfigMap or Secret, and depending on our deployment settings, Kubernetes can trigger a new rollout, or our application will reload the values at runtime.

ConfigMaps can also be mounted to a container as a set of files, so an application can access them from the filesystem, which is often required by legacy or third-party software. The same holds for Secrets, which are especially useful for SSL certificates, private keys, or other files that require strict permissions and handling.

Mounting configuration as files is now considered best practice, as it allows us to leverage the filesystem abstraction and keep applications agnostic to how configuration is provisioned. To illustrate, after creating a ConfigMap and adding it to an existing Deployment, we can verify visibility by executing into the Pod—the mounted files will appear in the container's filesystem, confirming successful injection without code changes.

The secure configuration management features of Kubernetes should always be deployed with proper access controls. Only those Pods and users that require access to a given Secret should be allowed to read it, and the use of encryption at rest should be activated in production clusters. Regular audits of Secret usage and automating secret rotation help protect our environment. Always use Secrets, not ConfigMaps, for anything confidential, and keep our configuration decoupled, centralized, and easy to update as our applications and our teams grow.

By structuring our clusters this way, we keep our Kubernetes workloads both flexible and secure, providing a foundation for robust application delivery in any environment.

Summary

In this chapter, we explored how to decouple configuration from container images using ConfigMaps and Secrets. We learned that ConfigMaps store nonsensitive key-value pairs and allow us to manage application settings, feature flags, and URLs outside of our code. We then examined Secrets, which provide base64 encoding, encryption at rest, and tmpfs-backed mounting to protect passwords, tokens, and certificates with stronger security guarantees. We discovered that mounting configuration as files is the modern best practice, as it leverages the filesystem abstraction and works seamlessly with legacy applications. Through practical examples, we verified that configuration injection happens transparently—our applications can access these values from the filesystem or environment without code changes. By securing our configuration management with proper RBAC rules and encryption, we create clusters that are both flexible and secure as our teams and applications scale.

In the next chapter, we will explore how Kubernetes helps us organize and manage the growing complexity of our clusters through labels, selectors, and annotations—the fundamental mechanisms that enable objects to discover and connect with each other automatically.

CHAPTER 11

Labels, Selectors, and Annotations

Introduction

As our Kubernetes clusters expand from simple demonstrations to complex production environments hosting numerous applications, managing and organizing all these resources becomes increasingly challenging. Kubernetes provides powerful mechanisms for organizing, selecting, and describing resources through labels, selectors, and annotations. These features form the foundation of how Kubernetes objects connect to each other and enable us to manage infrastructure efficiently across diverse workloads and environments.

Objectives

In this chapter, we explore three fundamental Kubernetes features that work together to organize and manage cluster resources:

- Understand how labels function as key-value pairs for categorizing and identifying resources across pods, services, and deployments

- Learn how selectors use labels to establish relationships between Kubernetes objects and automatically group related resources

- Discover how annotations provide additional metadata storage without affecting object selection or management

© Brando Marzio Sabatini 2026
B. M. Sabatini, *Kubernetes for Absolute Beginners*, https://doi.org/10.1007/979-8-8688-2445-6_11

- Apply labels and selectors to organize workloads by environment, application, and hardware characteristics

- Examine the relationship between services, labels, and endpoints that enables automatic traffic routing

As our Kubernetes clusters grow from simple demonstrations to complex production environments hosting numerous applications, organizing and managing all these resources becomes increasingly challenging. Kubernetes provides powerful mechanisms for organizing, selecting, and describing our resources through labels, selectors, and annotations. These features form the foundation of how Kubernetes objects connect to each other and how we can efficiently manage our infrastructure.

Labels are key-value pairs that we attach to Kubernetes objects such as pods, services, and deployments. Think of labels as sticky notes that can help categorize and identify our resources. Unlike names, which must be unique within a namespace, labels can be applied to multiple objects and are designed to be meaningful to users. For example, we might label our pods with information like environment: production, app: nginx, or version: v1.2.3.

The power of labels becomes apparent when we need to group related resources or perform operations on multiple objects simultaneously. Labels provide a flexible way to organize our workloads without having to know the specific names or locations of individual resources. This organizational system becomes essential as our applications scale and we need to manage hundreds or thousands of objects across multiple environments.

Looking at practical examples from our previous chapters, we have already seen labels in action. The ReplicaSet YAML file used labels to identify which pods it should manage. The selector field in the ReplicaSet specification used matchLabels to connect to pods with the app: nginx label. This connection between the ReplicaSet and its pods demonstrates how selectors work: they use labels to establish relationships between different Kubernetes objects.

Selectors are the mechanism that uses labels to identify and group objects. When we create a service, deployment, or ReplicaSet, we specify a selector that tells Kubernetes which pods or other resources the object should manage or connect to. The selector of a ClusterIP service connects directly to pods by matching their labels (e.g., app=nginx), and a Deployment manages pods through its ReplicaSet, which uses the same label selectors to control those pods. Together, this ensures Kubernetes can route traffic to the correct pods and maintain the desired number of replicas.

When we label a resource, existing pods that match those labels automatically become part of any new selector-based constructs we create. For example, if we have pods already running with the app=nginx label, we can immediately assign them to a Service by creating a selector that matches this label without needing to recreate or redeploy the pods (see Figure 11-1).

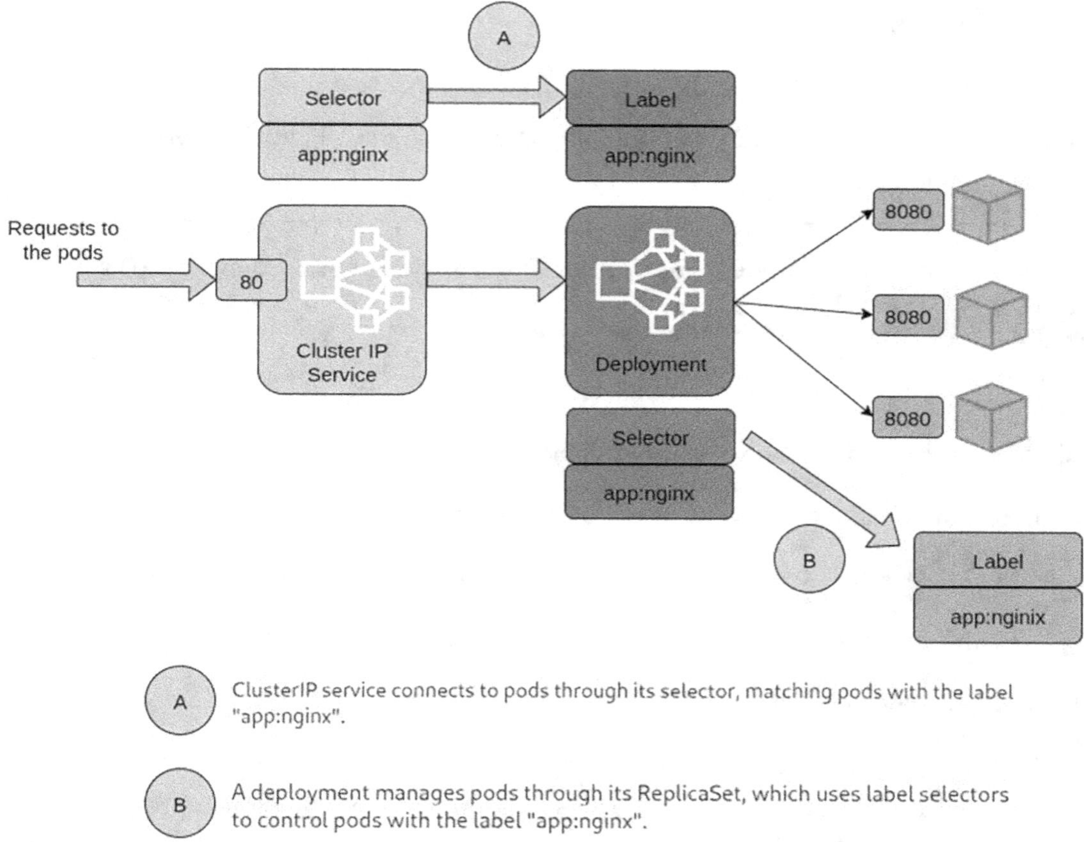

A   ClusterIP service connects to pods through its selector, matching pods with the label "app:nginx".

B   A deployment manages pods through its ReplicaSet, which uses label selectors to control pods with the label "app:nginx".

Figure 11-1. *This diagram shows how selectors use labels to connect services and deployments to their pods*

To see labels in action, we can display all pods with their labels using the command:

```
sudo kubectl get pods --show-labels
```

This command reveals the labels attached to each pod, helping us understand how our objects are organized. We can also filter pods based on specific labels:

```
sudo kubectl get pods -l app=nginx
```

This command shows only the pods that have the label app=nginx, demonstrating how selectors work in practice.

Labels also enable more sophisticated deployment strategies. We can deploy pods on specific nodes by using node labels and node selectors. First, we identify our available nodes:

```
sudo kubectl get nodes
```

Important   In the following commands, <node-name> should be replaced with the actual node's name.

Then we can label a node to indicate its characteristics, such as having SSD storage:

```
kubectl label node <node-name> ssd=true
```

If we need to change a node's label, we can overwrite it:

```
kubectl label node <node-name> disk=hdd --overwrite
```

To remove a label entirely, we use the minus sign:

```
kubectl label node <node-name> disk-
```

We can then query for nodes with specific labels:

```
kubectl get nodes -l disk=hdd
```

This labeling system allows us to ensure that pods requiring specific hardware characteristics, like fast storage or GPU acceleration, are scheduled on appropriate nodes. However, if all nodes with matching labels are offline, the pods may not be deployed until suitable nodes become available.

While labels are designed for organizing and selecting resources, annotations serve a different purpose. Annotations are also key-value pairs attached to objects, but they store non-identifying metadata that is not used for selection. Annotations typically contain larger amounts of data and are used to store information that tools and libraries need, such as build information, contact details, or configuration data for external systems.

The relationship between services and their endpoints demonstrates another important use of labels and selectors. When we create a service, Kubernetes automatically creates endpoints that list the IP addresses of pods matching the service's selector. We can examine these endpoints:

sudo kubectl get service

Then inspect a specific service to see its endpoints:

kubectl describe service nginx-service

The endpoints shown correspond to the IP addresses of pods that match the service's selector. We can verify this by checking the pod IP addresses:

sudo kubectl get pods -o wide

For each endpoint, the kube-proxy creates iptables rules with the IP address of the pod to properly forward requests to it. This automatic endpoint management relies entirely on the label-selector relationship between services and pods.

The EndpointSlice resource provides another view of how labels and selectors work together. We can examine these with:

sudo kubectl get endpointslice

The condition "ready: true" relates to the pod's ready state, and the maximum number of IP addresses in an EndpointSlice is defined by the parameter --max-endpoints-per-slice passed to the Kubernetes controller manager.

Understanding labels, selectors, and annotations is crucial for effective Kubernetes management. Labels provide the organizational structure, selectors create the relationships between objects, and annotations store additional metadata. Together, they enable us to build complex, scalable applications where components can find and communicate with each other automatically, regardless of how our cluster evolves over time.

Summary

Labels, selectors, and annotations form a powerful organizational system that underlies Kubernetes resource management. Labels serve as key-value pairs that help us categorize and identify resources across our cluster, enabling flexible organization without relying on hardcoded names. Selectors use these labels to establish relationships between Kubernetes objects, automatically grouping and connecting related resources such as pods to services and deployments. Annotations store additional non-identifying metadata that tools and external systems need, complementing labels by providing information that doesn't affect object selection. Together, these three mechanisms enable us to build complex, scalable applications where components find and communicate with each other automatically, regardless of how our cluster evolves over time. Understanding and effectively applying labels, selectors, and annotations is essential for managing production Kubernetes environments with clarity and efficiency.

In the next chapter, we will explore namespaces and how they provide logical isolation within our clusters. We will examine how namespaces create boundaries for security policies, resource allocation, and access control, and then learn practical strategies for implementing comprehensive namespace isolation using RBAC, network policies, and resource quotas.

CHAPTER 12

Exploring Namespaces

Introduction

As our Kubernetes usage grows from simple workloads to production-ready platforms, organizing and isolating resources inside the cluster becomes essential rather than optional. In this chapter, we shift our focus from individual pods and services to the higher-level structure that keeps them manageable: namespaces.

We will see how namespaces help us separate teams, environments, and applications within a single cluster, and how they become the natural boundary for applying security controls, resource limits, and access policies. Building on earlier concepts such as RBAC, network policies, and resource quotas, this chapter connects the theory of multitenancy with a practical, hands-on workflow for designing and operating namespaces in real environments.

Objectives

By the end of this chapter, we will be able to

- Explain how namespaces provide logical boundaries for organizing workloads in a Kubernetes cluster

- Describe how namespaces interact with RBAC, network policies, and resource quotas to enable secure multitenancy

- Understand how namespace scoping affects service discovery, naming, and resource visibility

© Brando Marzio Sabatini 2026

B. M. Sabatini, *Kubernetes for Absolute Beginners*, https://doi.org/10.1007/979-8-8688-2445-6_12

- Create, list, and manage namespaces using kubectl, including working within a specific namespace context

- Apply resource quotas at the namespace level to control CPU and memory consumption

As our Kubernetes journey progresses from basic pod management to production-ready deployments, organizing and securing our cluster resources becomes paramount. This chapter builds upon the foundational concepts we explored in Chapter 3, where we introduced namespaces as logical divisions within our cluster, and extends the security concepts touched upon in previous chapters (see Figure 12-1).

Figure 12-1. *This figure illustrates the core Linux kernel namespaces that our containers rely on for isolation*

While individual pods and services form the building blocks of our applications, namespaces provide the organizational structure that enables us to operate multiple projects, teams, or environments within a single cluster safely and efficiently.

Understanding namespace isolation involves recognizing that Kubernetes namespaces serve as more than simple organizational tools. They function as the primary boundary for implementing security policies, resource allocation controls, and access restrictions. When properly configured with role-based access control (RBAC) and network policies, namespaces create secure multi-tenant environments where different teams can operate independently without interfering with each other's workloads.

The concept of namespace isolation operates on multiple dimensions simultaneously. At the API level, Kubernetes enforces object name uniqueness within namespace boundaries while allowing identical names across different namespaces. This isolation extends to resource quotas, where administrators can allocate specific amounts of CPU, memory, and storage to each namespace, preventing resource starvation scenarios where one team's applications consume cluster resources needed by others (see Figure 12-2).

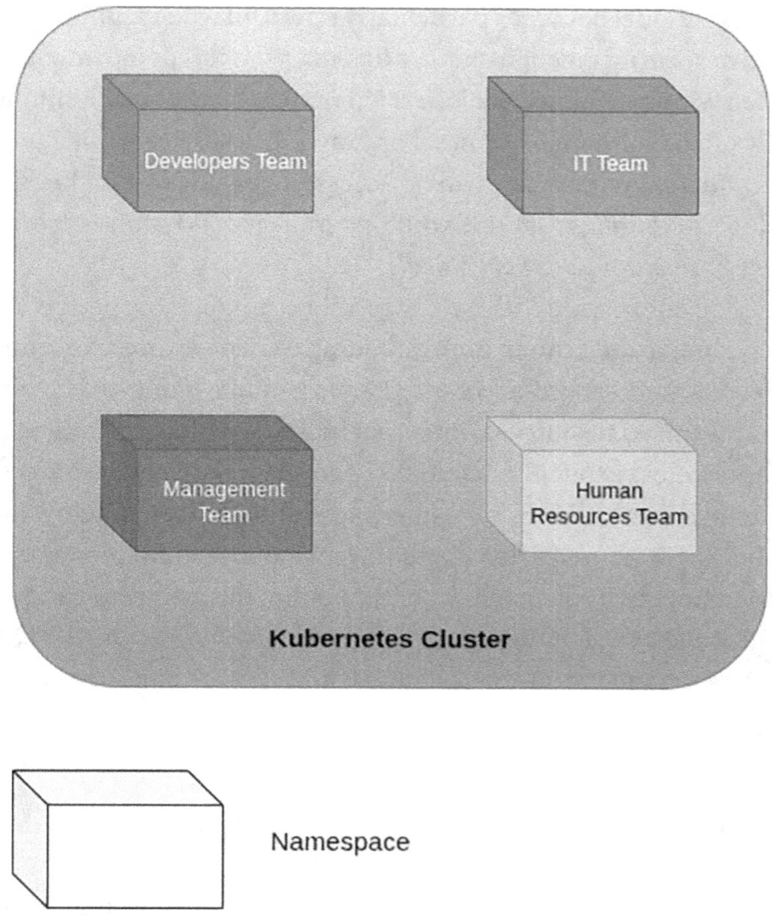

Figure 12-2. *This figure shows how different teams can share a single Kubernetes cluster while working in their own dedicated namespaces*

Understanding Namespace Boundaries

Modern Kubernetes deployments require sophisticated approaches to multitenancy and resource isolation. Organizations running production workloads typically need to separate development, staging, and production environments while ensuring that multiple teams can collaborate without creating conflicts or security vulnerabilities. Namespaces provide the foundation for this separation by creating logical boundaries that encapsulate related resources while maintaining a clear organizational structure.

The namespace model becomes particularly powerful when combined with Kubernetes' native security mechanisms. By default, services, deployments, and other resources created within a namespace can reference each other using simple names rather than fully qualified domain names. For example, a service named *database-service* in the production namespace can be accessed by pods within the same namespace using just *database-service*, while external access requires the full name *database-service.production.svc.cluster.local.*

Resource organization within namespaces follows predictable patterns that facilitate both automated tooling and human understanding. When we create resources like ConfigMaps, Secrets, and PersistentVolumeClaims within a namespace, they become available to all authorized resources within that boundary while remaining invisible to other namespaces unless explicitly shared through cluster-scoped resources.

Network communication between namespaces operates on an "allow by default" principle in standard Kubernetes installations. While pods in different namespaces can communicate freely without explicit configuration, this behavior can be restricted through network policies that implement zero-trust networking principles. This approach requires administrators to explicitly define allowed communication paths rather than relying on implicit trust relationships.

Practical Implementation Strategies

Implementing comprehensive namespace isolation requires coordinating multiple Kubernetes features, including RBAC, network policies, resource quotas, and certificate management. Successful implementations typically follow systematic approaches that address each isolation dimension while maintaining operational simplicity and avoiding configuration conflicts between different security mechanisms.

The implementation process typically begins with designing the namespace structure that reflects organizational boundaries, application relationships, and security requirements. This design should consider both current needs and future growth patterns to avoid requiring significant restructuring as the cluster scales. Common patterns include separating namespaces by environment (development, staging, production), by team or business unit, or by application lifecycle stage.

Establishing baseline security policies provides a foundation for namespace-specific configurations. These policies might include default network policies that implement zero-trust networking principles, standard RBAC roles that provide common permission patterns, and resource quotas that prevent resource exhaustion. Having consistent baseline policies across namespaces simplifies administration while ensuring that security requirements are met consistently.

Testing and validation procedures become essential when implementing complex namespace isolation configurations. Changes to network policies, RBAC rules, or resource quotas can have unexpected effects on application functionality, making systematic testing crucial for maintaining service availability. Implementation should include rollback procedures and monitoring systems that can detect configuration problems before they affect production workloads.

Regular auditing and maintenance of namespace configurations ensures that isolation controls remain effective as applications and requirements evolve. This includes reviewing RBAC permissions to remove unused access, updating network policies to accommodate new service communication patterns, and adjusting resource quotas based on observed usage patterns and changing application requirements.

Integration with external systems like identity providers, certificate authorities, and monitoring systems requires careful consideration of namespace boundaries and security implications. These integrations should maintain the isolation properties that namespaces provide while enabling necessary functionality for operations, security, and compliance requirements.

Creating and Managing Namespaces in Practice

Now that we understand the concepts behind namespaces, let's work through a practical example that demonstrates how to create, organize, and work with namespaces in our cluster. This hands-on approach will help us understand how namespaces function in real situations.

Setting Up Our Example Namespaces

Imagine we work for a company with different teams. We need to set up separate namespaces for our development team and production team. Let's start by creating these namespaces using kubectl.

First, let's create a namespace for development work. Type this command:

```
kubectl create namespace development
```

Next, let's create a namespace for production applications:

```
kubectl create namespace production
```

To verify that both namespaces have been created successfully, use this command to list all namespaces in our cluster:

```
kubectl get namespaces
```

We should see the four default namespaces, default, kube-system, kube-public and kube-node-lease, along with the new development and production namespaces we just created.

Working Within a Specific Namespace

By default, kubectl commands work with the default namespace. However, we can specify which namespace we want to work with by using the -n flag with our commands.

Let's create a simple pod in the development namespace. Type:

```
kubectl run web-server --image=nginx:latest -n development
```

This command creates a pod named web-server running the nginx container image in the development namespace. The -n development flag tells kubectl which namespace to use.

Now let's create the same pod in the production namespace:

```
kubectl run web-server --image=nginx:latest -n production
```

Notice that we used the same pod name, web-server, in both namespaces. This is permitted because namespaces provide separate boundaries. Within each namespace, object names must be unique, but identical names can exist in different namespaces.

To list pods in the development namespace, type:

```
kubectl get pods -n development
```

To list pods in the production namespace, type:

```
kubectl get pods -n production
```

To see all pods across all namespaces at once, we can use the -A flag:

```
kubectl get pods -A
```

Understanding Namespace Isolation Through Service Names

Let's create a simple service in each namespace to see how namespace isolation affects service discovery. First, expose the web server in the development namespace as a service:

```
kubectl expose pod web-server --port=80 --target-port=80 -n development
```

Now expose the pod in the production namespace:

```
kubectl expose pod web-server --port=80 --target-port=80 -n production
```

List the services in each namespace to confirm they were created:

```
kubectl get services -n development
kubectl get services -n production
```

Notice that both services are named web-server, but they exist in different namespaces. Pods within the development namespace can access the development web-server service simply by using the name web-server. However, if a pod in the development namespace needs to access the web-server service in the production namespace, it must use the fully qualified name: web-server.production.svc.cluster.local

Setting Our Default Namespace

Rather than typing -n development or -n production with every command, we can set a default namespace. This changes which namespace our kubectl commands target by default.

To set our default namespace to development, use the kubectl config command:

```
kubectl config set-context --current --namespace=development
```

After running this command, all subsequent kubectl commands will target the development namespace unless we specify a different one with the -n flag.

To verify our current context and namespace, type:

```
kubectl config view --minify
```

We can change back to the default namespace at any time:

```
kubectl config set-context --current --namespace=default
```

Applying Resource Quotas to Namespaces

Resource quotas help prevent one team from consuming all cluster resources. Let's create a resource quota for the development namespace to limit resource consumption.

Create a file containing a resource quota specification. We can think of this as describing the maximum resources that the development namespace can use. Within this file, we would define limits for CPU and memory. For example, the development namespace might be limited to a maximum of 10 CPU cores and 20 gigabytes of memory across all pods running in that namespace.

To apply a resource quota, we would create a YAML file that describes these limits, then use:

```
kubectl apply -f resource-quota.yaml -n development
```

This command applies the resource quota to the development namespace. Once applied, Kubernetes enforces these limits, preventing pods from being created if they would exceed the namespace's allocated resources.

To view the resource quotas in the development namespace:

```
kubectl describe resourcequota -n development
```

This shows us the limits we've set and how much of those resources are currently being used by pods in the namespace.

Cleaning Up Namespaces

When we're done working with a namespace and want to remove it along with all resources within it, simply delete the namespace:

```
kubectl delete namespace development
```

Be careful with this command, as deleting a namespace removes all resources contained within it immediately and without a confirmation prompt. Always double-check that the correct namespace name is specified before running this command.

Practical Considerations

In a real environment, we would typically organize namespaces by team, application, or environment stage. A company might have namespaces like backend-dev, backend-prod, frontend-dev, frontend-prod, and infra-tools. Each namespace would have its own resource quotas, access controls, and network policies that match the team's requirements.

As we plan our namespace structure, think about how many separate environments we need, which teams require their own namespaces, and what resource limits make sense for each namespace. The namespace structure we create becomes the foundation for organizing our entire cluster, so planning it carefully from the beginning helps avoid significant restructuring later.

Summary

In this chapter, we learned how namespaces give our Kubernetes cluster a clear organizational structure and act as isolation boundaries for teams, environments, and applications. We saw how they interact with RBAC, network policies, and resource quotas to provide secure multitenancy while sharing the same underlying infrastructure. Through practical kubectl examples, we created and managed namespaces, ran identical resources in separate namespaces, and controlled resource usage with quotas. This foundation prepares us to design clusters that remain manageable and secure as our workloads and teams continue to grow. In the next chapter, we will build on this foundation by exploring how to monitor the health and performance of our Kubernetes clusters using probes, metrics, logs, and simple monitoring tools.

CHAPTER 13

Monitoring Health and Performance

Introduction

Welcome to the world of observing our Kubernetes cluster. As our systems grow and serve real users, a critical question emerges: How do we know if everything is actually working? Without visibility into what our applications and infrastructure are doing, we operate blindly, discovering problems only when users complain or services fail.

Monitoring answers this question by providing the visibility we need. In this chapter, we will build the foundation for understanding cluster health, exploring why monitoring matters, learning how to check our applications' wellbeing, and discovering how to spot problems before they become serious failures.

Objectives

By the end of this chapter, you will be able to

- Understand why monitoring our Kubernetes cluster differs from monitoring physical systems

- Use health probes to signal application status to Kubernetes

- Access pod information and resource usage through simple kubectl commands

- Recognize the three monitoring data types: metrics, logs, and traces

- Implement basic monitoring best practices from day one

© Brando Marzio Sabatini 2026
B. M. Sabatini, *Kubernetes for Absolute Beginners*, https://doi.org/10.1007/979-8-8688-2445-6_13

Think of monitoring our Kubernetes cluster like keeping an eye on our car's dashboard while driving. Just as our car's dashboard shows important information like speed, fuel level, and engine temperature, Kubernetes monitoring tells us how our applications and cluster are performing. Without this information, we might not know when something is going wrong until it's too late.

In this chapter, we'll learn why monitoring matters for beginners, how to check if our applications are healthy using simple commands, what the basic monitoring tools do, and how to spot problems before they become serious issues.

Remember, we don't need to become a monitoring expert right away. Just like learning to drive, we start with the basics and gradually become more skilled over time.

Why Monitor Our Kubernetes Cluster?

Imagine we're running a small online store using Kubernetes. Our store has different parts: a website that customers see, a payment system, and a database that stores customer information. Without monitoring, we wouldn't know if the payment system is slow, if the website is using too much memory, or if the database is about to run out of space.

Monitoring helps us in several important ways. Early problem detection means we can spot issues before customers notice them, just like how a car's temperature gauge warns us before the engine overheats. Performance optimization helps us understand which parts of our application need more resources and which parts are wasting them, similar to monitoring our car's fuel efficiency. Troubleshooting becomes much easier when we have information about what was happening when something went wrong, like having a black box recorder for our applications. However, monitoring Kubernetes differs fundamentally from monitoring physical systems. When our computer's cooling fan starts spinning loudly, we hear it immediately—a direct physical signal. With Kubernetes pods, we cannot hear or see problems directly. Instead, we must interpret abstract metrics: a pod's CPU usage percentage, memory consumption trends, or network latency measurements. What appears as a simple fact, "this pod is using 85% CPU," requires us to investigate logs, check application code, and correlate multiple data points to understand the underlying issue. This indirection is why effective Kubernetes monitoring demands deliberate practice and systematic thinking.

As we discussed in previous chapters about pods and deployments, Kubernetes automatically restarts failing containers and replaces unhealthy pods. However, monitoring gives us the visibility to understand why these failures are happening and helps us prevent them in the future.

Effective monitoring operates across three levels. At the infrastructure level, we monitor nodes, the physical or virtual machines running our cluster, tracking resources like CPU and memory availability. At the application level, we monitor deployments and services, understanding how our applications behave. At the pod level, we observe individual containers. This creates a unique challenge: monitoring Kubernetes is fundamentally different from monitoring physical systems. With a car, a failing cooling fan produces immediate, tangible signs. With Kubernetes, detecting a pod's performance degradation requires interpreting abstract metrics like CPU usage percentages and memory thresholds. We're observing system behavior indirectly through data rather than physical symptoms.

Health Probes: Our Application's Heartbeat

As we saw briefly in Chapter 7 when discussing pod health, let's now dive deeper into this important monitoring concept. Health probes are like a doctor checking our pulse; they regularly verify that our applications are working correctly.

Kubernetes uses three types of health checks, each serving a different purpose. Liveness probes check if our application is still running properly. Think of this like checking if someone is still breathing. If the *liveness probe* fails, Kubernetes restarts the container, assuming something has gone wrong internally.

Readiness probes determine if our application is ready to receive traffic from users. This is like checking if a store is open for business. An application might be running but not yet ready to serve customers because it's still loading data or connecting to databases.

Startup probes verify that our application has started successfully. This is especially useful for applications that take a long time to start up. It's like giving a slow starter extra time to get ready before checking if they're working properly.

Here's a simple example of how these probes work in practice. When we deploy a web application pod, the startup probe gives it time to initialize. Once the startup probe succeeds, the readiness probe checks if the application can handle requests. Throughout the application's lifetime, the liveness probe continuously monitors its health (see Figure 13-1).

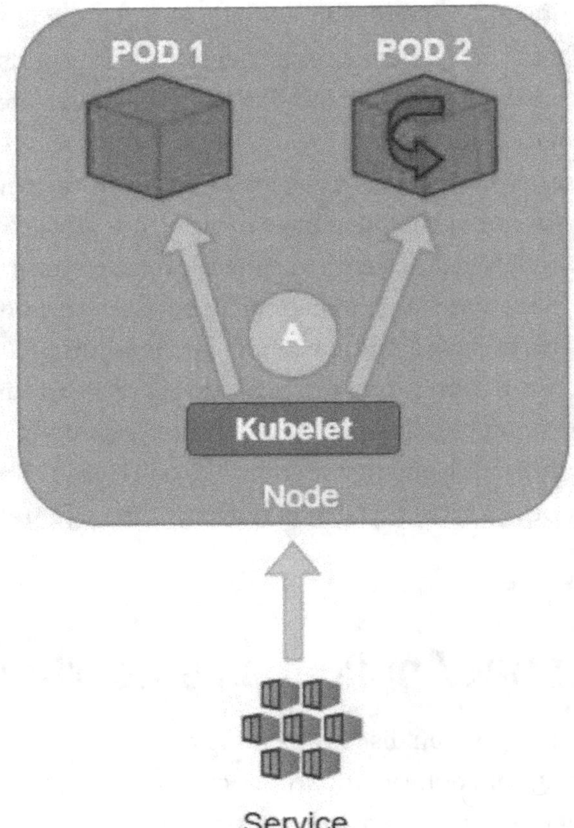

Figure 13-1. *Diagram of liveness probes restarting an unhealthy pod while traffic continues to the healthy pod*

Basic Monitoring with kubectl Commands

Pod Status and Resource Usage

The kubectl get pods command shows basic pod status, including restart counts and age. High restart counts typically indicate underlying problems requiring investigation.

For resource monitoring, use kubectl top commands (requires Metrics Server):

sudo kubectl top pods: Shows current CPU and memory usage per pod

sudo kubectl top nodes: Displays resource usage for each cluster node

Application Logs

Logs provide detailed records of application events, errors, and activities:

sudo kubectl logs pod-name: View pod logs

sudo kubectl logs pod-name -c container-name: Specify container in multi-container pods

sudo kubectl logs -f pod-name: Follow logs in real-time

sudo kubectl logs pod-name --tail=50: Show only recent log entries

The Metrics Server

The Metrics Server acts as our cluster's resource usage collector, gathering CPU and memory data every 15 seconds from each node. This data powers the kubectl top commands and enables automatic scaling features.

Most managed Kubernetes services include the Metrics Server by default. We can verify it's working by running **sudo kubectl top nodes**; if we see resource usage information, it's functioning correctly.

The Metrics Server stores only current data in memory and doesn't maintain historical information, making it lightweight and efficient for real-time monitoring.

Observability Fundamentals

Kubernetes monitoring relies on three key data types:

Metrics are numerical values showing system performance (CPU usage, memory consumption, response times, error rates). They answer "how fast?" and "how much?" questions.

Logs are detailed event records from our applications that reveal whether our system is running normally or abnormally, answering "what happened?" and "when did it occur?" questions.

Traces follow individual requests through multiple services, showing the complete journey and identifying bottlenecks in complex applications.

For beginners, focus on metrics and logs first. Traces become valuable as applications grow more complex with multiple interconnected services.

Monitoring Best Practices

Start with core metrics: monitor CPU usage, memory consumption, pod restart counts, and application response times. These reveal the most common problems.

- **Set up meaningful alerts:** Alert on critical issues like application downtime or resource exhaustion, but avoid alert fatigue from minor problems.

- **Understand normal patterns:** Learn our application's typical behavior—some use more CPU during business hours; others show gradual memory increases over time.

- **Keep initial monitoring simple:** Use built-in Kubernetes tools before adding complex monitoring solutions. This prevents overwhelming complexity while learning.

- **Document issues and solutions:** Record problem symptoms and resolutions to build a troubleshooting knowledge base.

Next Steps

Begin by regularly using **kubectl get pods** to check application health and **kubectl logs** to investigate issues. Get comfortable with **kubectl top** to understand resource usage patterns.

As we gain experience, explore cloud provider monitoring services for managed Kubernetes clusters, and consider learning about Prometheus and Grafana—these are popular open-source monitoring tools in the Kubernetes ecosystem.

Keep in mind that effective monitoring focuses on collecting the right data to solve real problems and improve user experience, not on gathering as much data as possible. The monitoring foundation we build now will become increasingly valuable as we work with more complex Kubernetes deployments.

Summary

Monitoring transforms our Kubernetes clusters from black boxes into transparent systems. We discovered that visibility operates at three levels: infrastructure monitoring tracks node resources, application monitoring observes deployments and services, and pod-level monitoring examines individual containers.

Health probes form the heartbeat of our applications. Liveness probes detect failures and trigger restarts. Readiness probes ensure traffic reaches only prepared containers. Startup probes give slow-starting applications time to initialize.

We explored how kubectl commands provide direct monitoring access without external tools. The kubectl get pods command reveals container status. The kubectl top commands show resource consumption. The kubectl logs commands record what our applications were doing when issues occurred.

In the next chapter, we will explore managing stateful and stateless applications, understanding how Kubernetes handles data persistence, and which tools to use for each type of workload.

CHAPTER 14

Stateful vs. Stateless Applications

Introduction

Welcome to another fundamental concept in Kubernetes. Throughout this book, we have been building our understanding of how Kubernetes works, from containers and pods to the tools Kubernetes provides for managing our applications. Now we arrive at a question that might seem simple on the surface but carries profound implications for how we design and deploy systems: Do applications need to remember things?

This question divides the entire world of applications into two distinct categories, and Kubernetes treats each one very differently. Some applications are designed to handle requests in complete isolation, forgetting everything once a request is processed. Other applications must retain information across multiple requests, remembering data even when they restart or move to different servers. Before we explore the specific Kubernetes tools for managing each type, it is vital to understand this fundamental distinction: What does it mean for an application to be stateful or stateless? How does this affect the way Kubernetes manages them? And why should we care about this difference from day one?

To make this distinction concrete, consider two real-world scenarios: A stateless web API that processes user requests independently without storing any session data, similar to a library reference desk where each visitor's query is answered from the current catalog without needing to recall who visited yesterday or what they previously asked for, will seamlessly recover when its pod crashes because a replacement pod can immediately take over with no data loss. In contrast, a stateful MySQL database managing critical business transactions must maintain its data across pod restarts and requires that when mysql-0 fails and gets replaced by Kubernetes, the new pod reconnects to the same PersistentVolume containing all existing records and state information, ensuring not a single transaction is lost.

In this chapter, we will introduce these two application categories with clear, concrete examples we can visualize and understand. This foundation will make every subsequent deployment decision easier and help us avoid common pitfalls that arise from misunderstanding how our application manages data.

Objectives

By the end of this chapter, we will be able to

- Define what stateful and stateless applications are and recognize the key differences between them

- Understand how Kubernetes Deployments excel at managing stateless workloads through their simplicity and scalability

- Recognize why stateful applications require specialized Kubernetes resources like StatefulSets and persistent storage mechanisms

- Identify real-world scenarios where choosing the right architecture prevents data loss, inconsistent behavior, and operational failures

- Comprehend the relationship between application state management, persistent volumes, and network identity in Kubernetes

Understanding the fundamental difference between stateful and stateless applications forms a cornerstone of effective Kubernetes deployment strategies. As we explored in previous chapters about pods and deployments, Kubernetes excels at managing different types of applications, but the approach varies significantly depending on whether our application needs to maintain persistent data or can operate independently with each request.

When building applications in Kubernetes, this distinction determines not only how we architect our solution but also which Kubernetes resources we should use to deploy and manage our workloads effectively. The choice between deploying a stateless web service using a Deployment or a stateful database using a StatefulSet can make the difference between a resilient, scalable application and one that experiences data loss or inconsistent behavior.

Understanding Stateless Applications

Stateless applications treat each incoming request as completely independent, without relying on any previously stored information or session data. Think of a stateless application like ordering at a fast food restaurant, where each order is processed independently, regardless of what we ordered yesterday or even five minutes earlier. The application contains no memory of past interactions.

In the context of Kubernetes, stateless applications typically include web servers, API gateways, load balancers, and microservices that process requests without storing any data locally. When a pod running a stateless application crashes and gets replaced by Kubernetes, the new pod can seamlessly take over without any concerns about losing important information. Each pod instance remains completely interchangeable with any other instance.

As we discussed in previous chapters about deployments, these applications work perfectly with standard Kubernetes Deployments because they scale horizontally with ease. When demand increases, Kubernetes can quickly spin up additional pod replicas, and when demand decreases, it can terminate pods without worrying about data preservation. The beauty of stateless applications lies in their simplicity for scaling operations.

Common examples of stateless workloads include content delivery services that serve static files, authentication services that validate tokens without storing session state, and RESTful APIs that process requests based solely on the information provided in each request. These applications often connect to external databases or storage services to retrieve the data they need for processing requests, but they do not maintain any persistent state within themselves.

Understanding Stateful Applications

Stateful applications, in contrast, require persistent storage and maintain information that must survive across pod restarts, updates, and scaling operations. These applications depend on data that accumulates over time and requires consistent access patterns. Database servers exemplify this perfectly, as they store critical business data that must persist even when the database pod crashes or gets rescheduled to a different node.

The complexity of stateful applications extends beyond simple data persistence. They often require stable network identities, meaning that other components in our system need to connect to specific instances using predictable hostnames or addresses. Consider a PostgreSQL database cluster where the primary database accepts write operations while replica databases handle read requests. Each database instance needs a stable identity so that applications know exactly which instance serves which role.

In previous chapters, we mentioned how Kubernetes automatically restarts failing containers and replaces unhealthy pods. With stateful applications, this process becomes more nuanced because the replacement pod must reconnect to the same persistent storage and potentially maintain the same network identity to preserve the application's functionality.

Stateful applications also frequently implement clustering or replication patterns where data synchronization occurs between different instances. These patterns require careful orchestration during startup, scaling, and shutdown operations to prevent data corruption or split-brain scenarios. The sequential nature of these operations means that scaling stateful applications takes more time and planning compared to their stateless counterparts.

To illustrate this persistence in action, consider a StatefulSet managing a MySQL instance where the pod mysql-0 mounts a PersistentVolume containing critical transaction logs and database files. If mysql-0 encounters a failure, Kubernetes detects the unhealthy pod and initiates a replacement, launching a new pod with the identical name mysql-0. This newly created pod automatically mounts the same PersistentVolume that stored the previous instance's data, seamlessly reconnecting to all existing records, indexes, and state information without any data loss or manual intervention. This capability distinguishes stateful management from stateless approaches, where losing a pod simply means losing that temporary container—with StatefulSets, the pod's identity and storage binding remain constant across the entire lifecycle of failures and replacements.

Key Differences in Kubernetes Management

Figure 14-1 shows a three-member StatefulSet in Kubernetes, where each pod ("stateful-0," "stateful-1," "stateful-2") runs on a master or worker node and is bound to its own persistent volume. Green arrows indicate pods reading data from their volumes, the red arrow shows a pod writing data to its volume, and purple circular arrows represent data synchronization between volumes to keep them consistent.

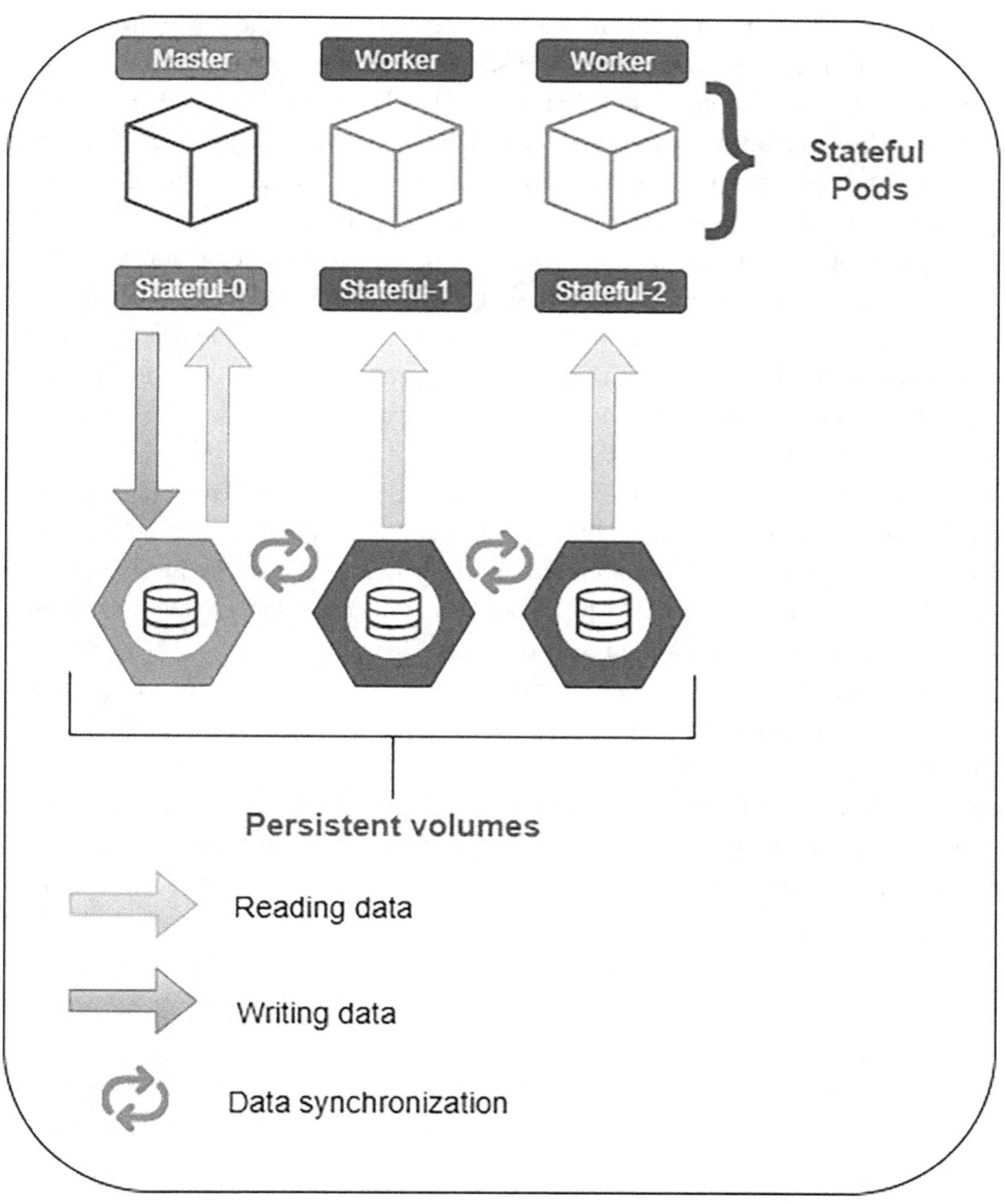

Figure 14-1. *StatefulSet data replication and storage*

The management approaches for stateful and stateless applications in Kubernetes differ dramatically across several dimensions. Pod identity represents one of the most significant distinctions. Stateless applications use Deployments that create pods with random, generated names like web-app-7c6d9f8b4d-xk2m7. When these pods fail or get replaced, Kubernetes simply creates new pods with different random names, and this approach works perfectly because the pods remain interchangeable.

Stateful applications managed by StatefulSets receive stable, predictable names following a pattern like database-0, database-1, database-2. These names persist even when pods get rescheduled or restarted, ensuring that other components can reliably connect to specific instances. This naming stability proves essential for applications that require direct pod-to-pod communication or where external systems need to maintain connections to particular instances.

Storage handling reveals another fundamental difference. Stateless applications typically use ephemeral storage that disappears when pods terminate, or they connect to external storage services without maintaining persistent volumes themselves. StatefulSets, however, automatically provision and manage persistent volumes for each pod instance, ensuring that data survives pod lifecycle events.

Scaling behavior also differs significantly between the two approaches. Deployments can scale stateless applications instantly, creating or destroying multiple pods simultaneously without coordination concerns. StatefulSets enforce ordered scaling, creating pods sequentially and waiting for each pod to become ready before proceeding to the next. This sequential approach prevents race conditions and ensures that clustering or replication protocols can establish proper relationships between instances.

When to Choose Each Approach

Table 14-1 summarizes the key differences between stateless and stateful applications across several operational dimensions.

Table 14-1. *Stateless vs. stateful applications comparison*

Aspect	Stateless apps	Stateful apps
Pod naming	Random names (web-app-xxx)	Ordered names (db-0, db-1, db-2)
Storage	Ephemeral or external storage	Persistent volumes auto-provisioned
Scaling	Instant parallel scaling	Sequential scaling with readiness
Network	Dynamic IPs interchangeable	Stable network identities and DNS
Updates	Rolling updates; rapid replacement	Ordered updates respecting deps
Use cases	Web servers, APIs, microservices	Databases, queues, file systems
Kubernetes resource	Deployment with ReplicaSet	StatefulSet with ordered mgmt
Recovery	Fast—instant replacement	Slower—data consistency required
Complexity	Low—simple to manage	High—specialized expertise needed

The decision between stateless and stateful deployment strategies depends on our application's fundamental characteristics and requirements. Choose stateless deployments when your application processes requests independently, stores no local data, scales horizontally without coordination requirements, and can tolerate rapid pod replacement without service disruption.

Web applications that serve static content, microservices that transform data without storing state, API gateways that route requests, and load balancers represent ideal candidates for stateless deployment. These applications benefit from the rapid scaling, simple updates, and fault tolerance that Deployments provide.

Select stateful deployments for applications that maintain persistent data, require stable network identities, implement clustering or leader election patterns, or need ordered startup and shutdown sequences. Database systems, message queues, distributed caches, and file storage systems typically require StatefulSet management to function correctly in Kubernetes environments.

Modern applications often combine both approaches within the same system. A typical e-commerce platform might use stateless Deployments for the web frontend and API services while relying on StatefulSets for the underlying database clusters and search engines. This hybrid architecture leverages the strengths of each deployment type while maintaining overall system reliability.

Production Considerations

As Kubernetes continues evolving, several trends influence how organizations approach stateful and stateless application management. Dynamic Resource Allocation, which reached beta status in recent Kubernetes versions, enables more sophisticated resource management for both application types, particularly benefiting stateful workloads that require specialized hardware or exclusive device access.

Container Storage Interface enhancements have improved the reliability and performance of persistent storage for stateful applications, while networking improvements benefit stateless applications through more efficient load balancing and service discovery. Cloud provider integrations have also simplified the operational complexity of managing persistent volumes and backup strategies for stateful workloads.

Security considerations have become increasingly important, with both application types benefiting from improved admission controllers, network policies, and runtime security features. However, stateful applications often require additional security planning around data encryption, access controls, and backup procedures that stateless applications can typically avoid.

The operational complexity of managing stateful applications in production environments requires specialized skills in areas like backup and recovery planning, storage performance optimization, and disaster recovery procedures. Organizations must invest in training and tooling to successfully manage stateful workloads, while stateless applications generally require less specialized operational expertise.

Understanding these fundamental differences between stateful and stateless applications enables us to make informed architectural decisions and choose the appropriate Kubernetes resources for each component of our system. As we progress in our Kubernetes journey, this knowledge will guide us toward building more resilient, scalable, and maintainable applications.

Summary

The distinction between stateful and stateless applications forms the backbone of an effective Kubernetes deployment strategy. While stateless applications offer the simplicity, speed, and elasticity that make Kubernetes powerful, stateful applications require the structured guarantees that StatefulSets and persistent storage provide. Understanding which approach our application demands prevents costly mistakes from unnecessary data loss to over-engineered complexity. The choice we make here cascades through our entire architecture, influencing everything from scaling patterns to disaster recovery procedures.

As we build applications for Kubernetes, remember that statefulness is not a weakness or limitation; it is a characteristic that demands respect and careful design. By acknowledging this reality and selecting appropriate Kubernetes resources, we create systems that are both resilient and predictable.

Having understood how to manage data and application persistence, the next challenge is protecting access to that data and controlling who can interact with our cluster. Chapter 15 shifts our focus to Security in Kubernetes, where we will explore how to implement role-based access control (RBAC) to govern user and service account permissions, enforce network isolation through security policies to prevent unauthorized communication between applications, and establish certificate authorities that secure communication pathways within and outside our cluster. These security mechanisms work together to create defended environments where data remains protected, cluster resources stay isolated from unauthorized access, and compliance requirements are maintained as essential safeguards as our Kubernetes infrastructure grows more complex and critical to our operations.

CHAPTER 15

Security in Kubernetes

Introduction

This chapter examines security mechanisms within Kubernetes environments and the architectural controls that protect cluster resources. Security in Kubernetes operates across multiple integrated layers, from access control policies to network isolation to certificate management, each contributing to the overall security posture of deployed applications. We explore how role-based access control (RBAC) governs what users and workloads can access, how service accounts provide identity for applications, and how these systems interact with namespace boundaries and resource management. The relationship between different security components demonstrates that effective protection requires not isolated controls but coordinated strategies that align with operational requirements.

Objectives

This chapter enables us to

- Understand how RBAC enforces access control through roles and bindings within namespaced and cluster-wide scopes

- Implement service account strategies that establish pod identities and control their API server interactions

- Design network policies that manage pod-to-pod communication and prevent unauthorized cross-namespace traffic

B. M. Sabatini, *Kubernetes for Absolute Beginners*, https://doi.org/10.1007/979-8-8688-2445-6_15

- Recognize how ReplicaSet management contributes to security through consistent pod configuration and replica monitoring

- Integrate certificate authorities for secure service communication and mutual TLS (Transport Layer Security) authentication

Implementing Access Control Through RBAC

Role-based access control represents the primary mechanism for controlling access to namespace resources in Kubernetes. Unlike traditional access control systems that grant permissions to individual users, RBAC operates through a combination of roles that define permissions and bindings that associate those roles with users, groups, or service accounts. This model provides granular control over who can perform which operations on specific resources within namespace boundaries.

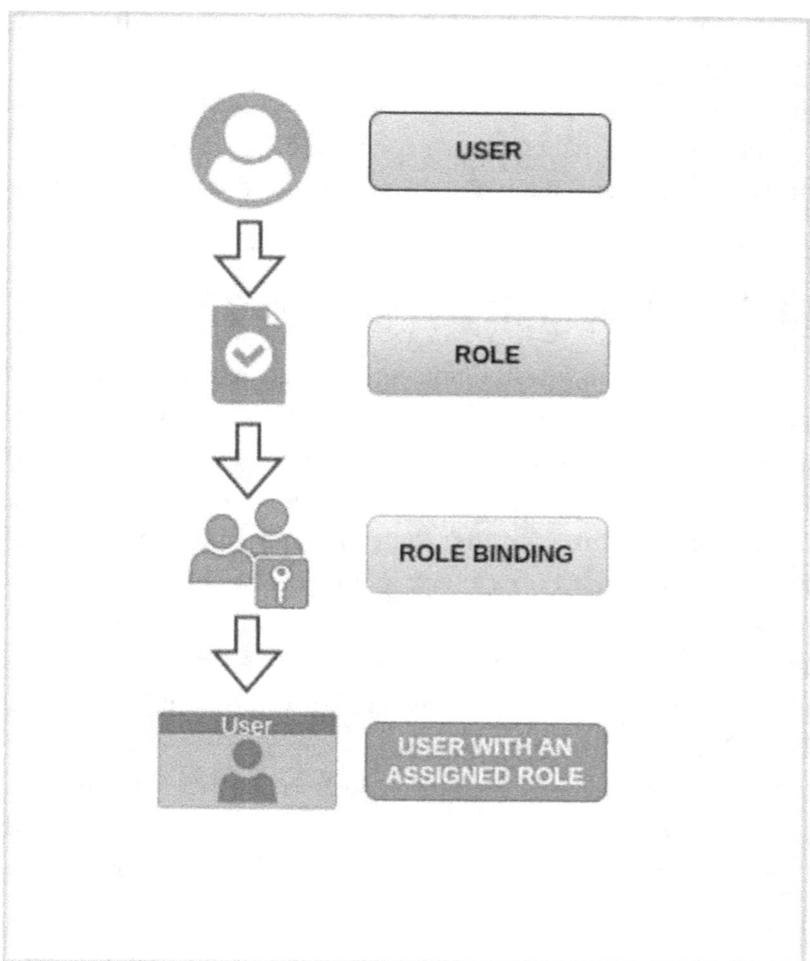

Figure 15-1. *This figure illustrates the RBAC authorization flow where a user is assigned a role through a role binding, ultimately granting the user specific permissions to perform actions on cluster resources*

Creating effective RBAC policies requires understanding the relationship between namespaced and cluster-scoped resources. While roles and role bindings operate within specific namespaces, cluster roles and cluster role bindings provide permissions across the entire cluster. When designing access control policies, administrators must carefully consider which permissions should be confined to specific namespaces versus those that require cluster-wide access.

The principle of least privilege forms the cornerstone of effective RBAC implementation. Rather than granting broad permissions that might be convenient in the short term, production deployments should provide users and service accounts with the minimum permissions required to perform their specific functions. This approach reduces the potential impact of security breaches while maintaining operational efficiency (see Figure 15-1).

Pod Identities Through Service Accounts

Service accounts play a crucial role in namespace-based access control by providing identity for applications and automated processes. Each namespace includes a default service account that provides basic permissions for pods running within that namespace. However, production applications typically require custom service accounts with specifically tailored permissions that align with their operational requirements.

A service account maps to a ServiceAccount object in Kubernetes and authenticates pods to the API server. When a pod authenticates as a particular service account, its level of access to cluster resources depends directly on the RBAC policies bound to that service account. This connection between identity and permissions creates the foundation for pod-level access control.

Creating a custom service account for our workload begins with defining a ServiceAccount object. For example, we might create a service account for an application that needs to interact with the Kubernetes API to monitor pod status or manage configuration resources.

```
apiVersion: v1
kind: ServiceAccount
metadata:
  name: app-reader
  namespace: production
```

Once the service account exists, we assign it to pods by specifying the serviceAccountName field in the pod specification. The pod then uses the credentials from this service account to authenticate with the API server.

```
apiVersion: v1
kind: Pod
metadata:
  name: app-pod
```

```
namespace: production
spec:
  serviceAccountName: app-reader
  containers:
  - name: app
    image: my-app:latest
```

Kubernetes automatically mounts the service account credentials as a volume within the pod. The credentials include a token that the pod's application can use to authenticate API requests. From version 1.22 onwards, Kubernetes enables the Bound Service Account Token Volume feature by default, so service account tokens are typically short-lived, audience-bound, and automatically rotated. This significantly reduces the impact window if a token is compromised.

Granting Pod Permissions Through RBAC

After assigning a service account to a pod, we must define RBAC permissions that determine what resources the service account can access. A Role defines a set of permissions within a specific namespace, while a ClusterRole defines permissions across the entire cluster.

Consider an application that needs to read pod information and configuration data from ConfigMaps within its namespace. We would create a Role that specifies these exact permissions.

app-reader-role.yaml

```
apiVersion: rbac.authorization.k8s.io/v1
kind: Role
metadata:
  name: app-reader-role
  namespace: production
rules:
- apiGroups: [""]
  resources: ["pods"]
  verbs: ["get", "list", "watch"]
- apiGroups: [""]
  resources: ["configmaps"]
  verbs: ["get"]
```

The rules section defines which resources the role can access and which actions (verbs) are permitted. The API group indicates which Kubernetes API group contains the resource. An empty string represents the core API group, while other resources like deployments belong to the "apps" API group.

To apply these permissions to the service account, we create a RoleBinding that connects the role to the service account.

`app-reader-binding.yaml`

```
apiVersion: rbac.authorization.k8s.io/v1
kind: RoleBinding
metadata:
  name: app-reader-binding
  namespace: production
roleRef:
  apiGroup: rbac.authorization.k8s.io
  kind: Role
  name: app-reader-role
subjects:
- kind: ServiceAccount
  name: app-reader
  namespace: production
```

Now the pod running with the app-reader service account can list and watch pods and read ConfigMaps within the production namespace. Any attempt to perform actions not included in the role rules, such as deleting pods or reading secrets, will be denied by the API server.

For workloads that need permissions across multiple namespaces or cluster-wide, we use ClusterRole and ClusterRoleBinding instead. A common scenario involves a monitoring application that needs to read pod metrics from all namespaces.

`metrics-reader.yaml`

```yaml
apiVersion: rbac.authorization.k8s.io/v1
kind: ClusterRole
metadata:
  name: metrics-reader
rules:
- apiGroups: [""]
  resources: ["pods"]
  verbs: ["get", "list"]
- apiGroups: [""]
  resources: ["pods/log"]
  verbs: ["get"]
```

This ClusterRole can be bound to a service account through a ClusterRoleBinding, granting the service account access to pods and pod logs throughout the entire cluster.

Table 15-1 shows the relationship between ReplicaSet security operations and the RBAC permissions required (see Figure 15-2).

Table 15-1. *Demonstrates the RBAC permissions required to perform common ReplicaSet management operations on pods and ReplicaSets*

ReplicaSet operation	API resource	Verbs required	Example role rule
List existing pods	pods	get, list, watch	apiGroups: [""] resources: ["pods"] verbs: ["get","list","watch"]
Create new pod replicas	pods	create	apiGroups: [""] resources: ["pods"] verbs: ["create"]
Update pod template (rolling)	replicasets	update, patch	apiGroups: ["apps"] resources: ["replicasets"] verbs: ["update","patch"]
Delete excess pods	pods	delete	apiGroups: [""] resources: ["pods"] verbs: ["delete"]

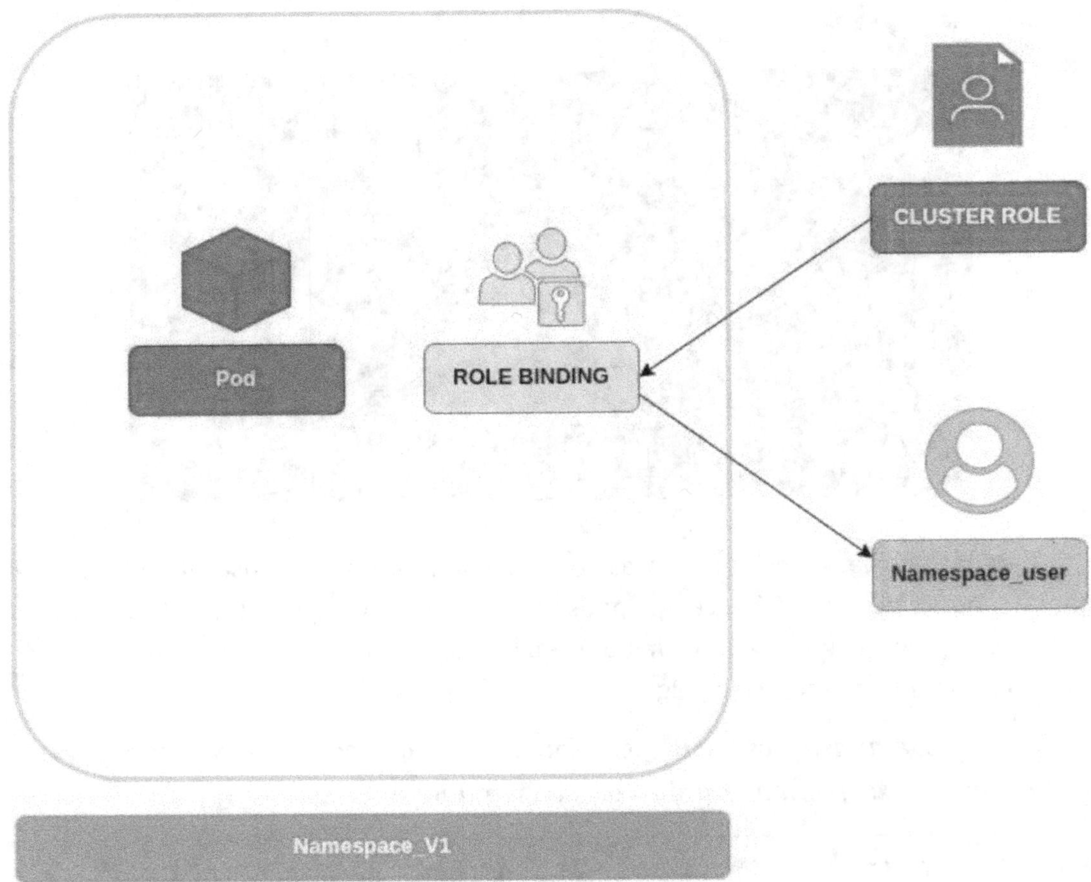

Figure 15-2. *This diagram shows how role bindings connect cluster roles and namespace users to pods within a namespace, establishing the access control relationships that govern resource permissions*

To demonstrate practical RBAC implementation, consider a scenario where development teams need read-write access to their designated namespaces while maintaining read-only access to shared service namespaces. This configuration requires creating roles that define appropriate permissions and then binding those roles to team members through groups or individual user accounts.

A typical role for development team access might include permissions to create, read, update, and delete pods, services, deployments, and ConfigMaps within their assigned namespace while explicitly excluding access to secrets or persistent volumes that might contain sensitive data. The role definition would specify these permissions through rules that identify API groups, resources, and allowed verbs.

Service Account Token Management

Kubernetes manages service account tokens automatically, but understanding the token lifecycle is important for security. When a pod is created with a service account, Kubernetes generates a token and mounts it as a volume at /var/run/secrets/kubernetes.io/serviceaccount/token. The token is a JWT that the application can use in API requests by including it as a Bearer token in the Authorization header.

For external systems that need to authenticate as a Kubernetes service account, we can manually create service account tokens using the TokenRequest API. This allows us to issue temporary credentials for specific use cases without storing long-lived secrets.

Applications should never be configured with hardcoded service account tokens. Instead, they should use the automatically mounted token from the service account volume. This approach ensures tokens are managed by Kubernetes and can be rotated without application changes.

Network Isolation and Security Policies

Network security within Kubernetes clusters extends beyond traditional firewall concepts to encompass pod-to-pod communication, service discovery, and external connectivity. While namespaces provide logical boundaries for organizing resources, network policies implement the technical controls that enforce communication restrictions between those boundaries. Understanding how network policies interact with namespace isolation enables administrators to create secure multi-tenant environments that maintain both functionality and security.

The default networking model in Kubernetes allows all pods to communicate with all other pods regardless of namespace boundaries. This permissive approach facilitates development and testing but creates security risks in production environments where different applications or tenants should not have unrestricted access to each other's resources. Network policies address this concern by implementing ingress and egress rules that define allowed communication paths.

Implementing network isolation typically begins with creating default deny policies that block all communication within a namespace, then systematically adding allow rules that permit required traffic flows. This approach ensures that new applications deployed to the namespace operate within defined security boundaries rather than having unrestricted network access that might violate security requirements.

Namespace-level network isolation becomes particularly important when hosting multiple applications or tenants within a single cluster. By implementing policies that restrict cross-namespace communication to explicitly authorized paths, administrators can prevent data leakage, reduce attack surfaces, and maintain compliance with security frameworks that require network segmentation.

Consider implementing network policies that allow communication within a namespace while blocking external access except through designated ingress points. This configuration enables applications within a namespace to communicate freely with their dependencies while preventing unauthorized access from other namespaces or external sources.

Advanced network segmentation scenarios might require implementing policies that allow communication between specific namespaces while blocking others. For example, applications in a frontend namespace might need access to services in a backend namespace while being prohibited from communicating with resources in a database namespace directly. These policies require careful planning and testing to ensure they provide security benefits without breaking application functionality.

Security Through Controlled Resource Management

When implementing security measures in Kubernetes environments, the management of workload replicas becomes a critical component that extends beyond simple availability concerns, as we explored in Chapter 8 with Deployments and ReplicaSets. These controllers provide more than just pod lifecycle management; by enforcing a consistent pod specification and replica count, they contribute to the overall security posture of our cluster. They are not a primary security boundary like RBAC or Pod Security admission, but they help ensure that workloads run with a uniform, policy-compliant configuration.

The security implications of ReplicaSets manifest through their selector-based pod management system. When a ReplicaSet maintains a specified number of pod replicas, it continuously monitors the cluster state to ensure that only pods matching the ReplicaSet's label selector remain active. This automatic reconciliation process ensures the correct number of matching pod replicas within our namespace: pods that match the label selector but exceed the specified replica count will be terminated, while pods that do not match the label selector remain unmanaged.

Resource quotas work in conjunction with ReplicaSet specifications to prevent privilege escalation through resource exhaustion attacks. By combining namespace-level resource limits with carefully configured replica counts, administrators can ensure that no single workload can consume excessive cluster resources, even if an attacker gains access to modify ReplicaSet configurations. The relationship between the controllers we discussed in Chapter 5, particularly the ReplicaSet controller within the controller manager, and these security boundaries demonstrates how Kubernetes security operates through multiple layers of control plane validation.

Pod Security Standards Integration

The Pod Security Standards framework integrates directly with ReplicaSet templates to enforce security policies at the workload level. When a ReplicaSet creates new pods from its template specification, each pod must comply with the security policies defined for its namespace. This enforcement occurs during the pod creation process, where the admission controllers validate the pod specification against the established security standards before allowing the ReplicaSet controller to schedule the pod.

Security contexts defined within ReplicaSet pod templates establish the foundation for container-level security controls. These contexts specify user identifiers, group memberships, security capabilities, and file system access modes that apply to every pod replica created by the controller. Unlike standalone pods that might be created with inconsistent security settings, ReplicaSets ensure uniform security configuration across all replicas, reducing the attack surface through standardized security policies.

The interaction between RBAC policies and ReplicaSet management creates additional security layers through controlled access to scaling operations. RBAC policies determine which users and automated systems can create, update, and delete ReplicaSets and the pods they manage within their designated namespaces. This permission model, when combined with the namespace isolation concepts from Chapter 12, ensures that workloads can only affect resources within their authorized scope, preventing lateral movement between different applications or environments within the same cluster.

Network Security Through Replica Distribution

Network policies gain effectiveness when applied to ReplicaSet-managed workloads because they can target all pod replicas through consistent labeling schemes. As we covered in Chapter 11 with labels and selectors, the label-based identification system allows network policies to automatically apply to new pod replicas as they're created, maintaining security boundaries without requiring manual intervention for each pod instance. This automatic policy application ensures that security controls scale seamlessly with application demands.

The distribution of pod replicas across cluster nodes introduces both security opportunities and challenges. While spreading replicas across multiple nodes reduces the impact of node-level security incidents, it also expands the potential attack surface. Implementing node-level security controls, including proper kubelet configuration and container runtime security measures, becomes essential when ReplicaSets distribute workloads throughout the cluster infrastructure.

Certificate Authority Setup for Namespace Security

Managing certificate authorities within Kubernetes namespaces requires understanding how TLS certificates interact with service communication and external access patterns. While Kubernetes provides built-in certificate management for cluster components, applications often require custom certificates for secure communication with external services or for implementing mutual TLS (mTLS) authentication between services within the cluster.

Certificate management strategies vary based on security requirements, operational complexity, and integration needs with existing certificate infrastructure. Organizations with established public key infrastructure might need to integrate their existing certificate authorities with Kubernetes certificate management systems, while others might implement cluster-local certificate authorities that provide certificates only for internal service communication.

The certificate authority model within Kubernetes supports multiple approaches ranging from simple self-signed certificates for development environments to sophisticated certificate hierarchies that integrate with external certificate authorities for production deployments. Understanding these options enables administrators to select appropriate certificate management strategies that balance security requirements with operational complexity.

Service mesh technologies like Linkerd and Istio provide automated certificate management capabilities that can simplify mTLS implementation within and across namespace boundaries. These systems typically implement their own certificate authorities that automatically provision certificates for services and handle certificate rotation without requiring manual intervention.

When implementing custom certificate authorities for namespace-specific applications, administrators must consider certificate distribution, rotation, and validation requirements. Certificates issued by namespace-local certificate authorities might not be trusted by services in other namespaces unless explicit trust relationships are established through shared certificate authority certificates or cross-signing arrangements.

Modern certificate management solutions like cert-manager provide Kubernetes-native approaches to certificate lifecycle management that can integrate with various certificate authorities, including Let's Encrypt for public certificates and internal certificate authorities for private service communication. These tools can automatically provision certificates based on annotations or custom resources, reducing the operational overhead of manual certificate management.

Summary

Security in Kubernetes depends on multiple coordinated mechanisms that work together to protect cluster resources and enforce authorization boundaries. Role-based access control provides the foundation through roles that define permissions and bindings that associate those roles with identities. Service accounts establish pod identity and determine what resources applications can access through their RBAC assignments. Network policies extend security beyond individual resources to manage communication paths between pods and enforce logical boundaries between namespaces. ReplicaSet controllers contribute to security by ensuring consistent pod configurations across replicas and ensuring consistent pod configuration across all replicas. Certificate authorities enable secure communication both within the cluster through mutual TLS and with external systems through certificate management solutions. Together, these mechanisms create defense-in-depth security that protects against unauthorized access, lateral movement, and data exposure while maintaining the operational flexibility required for cloud-native applications.

In the next chapter, we explore persistent storage solutions that enable applications to preserve data beyond pod restarts, examining how Persistent Volumes, Claims, and Storage Classes work together to provide durable data management in Kubernetes clusters.

CHAPTER 16

Storage Solutions in Kubernetes

Introduction

As our Kubernetes exploration moves from simple demo workloads to real applications, we inevitably face a crucial question: what happens to our data when pods are created, destroyed, or rescheduled? A container restart is harmless for a stateless web front end, but it becomes catastrophic for a database, a file-sharing service, or an AI pipeline that depends on durable data.

In this chapter, we focus on how Kubernetes, and specifically our K3s cluster, handles data that must outlive individual pods and nodes. We contrast ephemeral storage with persistent storage, introduce the core building blocks PersistentVolumes, PersistentVolumeClaims, and StorageClasses, and show how they work together to provide reliable, repeatable storage for stateful workloads. Along the way, we connect the concepts to practical YAML examples so that storage becomes another routine part of how we design and operate our clusters. Our goal is to move from "pods that lose everything on restart" to "applications that keep their state safely, no matter how often the cluster changes," using modern dynamic provisioning as the default, while still understanding the legacy static approach when it is required.

Objectives

By the end of this chapter, we will be able to

- Distinguish between ephemeral volumes (such as emptyDir) and persistent storage, and understand when each is appropriate

© Brando Marzio Sabatini 2026
B. M. Sabatini, *Kubernetes for Absolute Beginners*, https://doi.org/10.1007/979-8-8688-2445-6_16

- Explain the roles of PersistentVolumes (PVs), PersistentVolumeClaims (PVCs), and StorageClasses in the Kubernetes storage model

- Configure static (manually created) PersistentVolumes and bind them to PVCs in a K3s cluster

- Use dynamic provisioning with StorageClasses, including the default local-path provisioner in K3s, to automatically create storage on demand

- Mount storage into pods using PVCs and verify that data survives pod restarts and rescheduling

- Integrate network storage (such as NFS) with Kubernetes and understand when to expose it directly versus through PVs and PVCs

- Apply appropriate reclaim policies and clean-up procedures so that storage lifecycles align with our application and data-retention requirements

As our Kubernetes journey progresses from running simple nginx pods to building real applications, we'll encounter a fundamental challenge: what happens to our data when pods restart? Remember the nginx deployment we created in our YAML chapter? When that pod restarts, any files created inside the container disappear completely.

This works fine for stateless applications like web servers, but what about applications that need to store data permanently? Think about a blog where users upload photos or a database that stores user information. Without persistent storage, all that valuable data would vanish every time a pod restarts.

Dynamic Storage with Storage Classes: A Modern Approach

Kubernetes provides a powerful storage system that works in two complementary ways. For most applications, we'll use the automatic approach that K3s handles out-of-the-box. Let us see how it works.

When we request storage through a Persistent Volume Claim (PVC), K3s examines our request against available storage classes. A StorageClass is a template that defines what type of storage to provision and how to manage its lifecycle. K3s ships with a default local-path storage class already configured, which automatically creates storage on our cluster nodes.

Think of it this way: instead of manually building storage (like manually creating a USB drive and handing it to Kubernetes), we submit a request for storage, and K3s automatically builds exactly what we need. This is dynamic provisioning; it eliminates tedious manual setup and aligns with how modern Kubernetes deployments operate.

Let's see this in action by creating a storage request:

Create the claim and watch Kubernetes automatically provision storage:

```
sudo kubectl apply -f dynamic-storage.yaml
kubectl get pvc
kubectl get pv
```

Watch the transformation happen in real time. The PVC transitions from "Pending" to "Bound," and notice how Kubernetes automatically created a corresponding PersistentVolume. This is the efficiency of dynamic provisioning—no manual volume creation required. The local-path provisioner handles everything automatically based on the StorageClass definition.

Understanding Persistent Volumes and Claims

To understand what happened behind the scenes when we created that claim, let's explore the concepts.

A Persistent Volume (PV) is storage that exists independently of any pod. Think of it like a USB drive that persists even when no computer is connected to it. A Persistent Volume Claim (PVC) is how pods request access to that storage—it's a reservation request that says, "I need 1GB of storage with read-write access."

When we create a PVC, Kubernetes performs the binding process: it finds an available PV that matches our request (or automatically creates one using a StorageClass) and connects our claim to that volume. Once bound, any pod using that PVC gains access to the underlying storage.

Here's the binding relationship in practice:

pod-using-storage.yaml

```yaml
apiVersion: v1
kind: Pod
metadata:
  name: data-app
spec:
  containers:
  - name: app
    image: nginx:latest
    volumeMounts:
    - name: data-volume
      mountPath: /data
  volumes:
  - name: data-volume
    persistentVolumeClaim:
      claimName: app-data
```

Apply this pod alongside our PVC:

```
sudo kubectl apply -f pod-using-storage.yaml
kubectl get pods
kubectl describe pod data-app
```

Our pod is now using the dynamically provisioned storage. This demonstrates the complete flow: StorageClass → Automatic PV provisioning → PVC binding → Pod consumption.

Advanced Provisioning: Explicit StorageClass Control

While K3s automatically uses its default StorageClass when we omit the storageClassName field, explicitly specifying the storage class provides clarity and ensures consistent behavior across different clusters. Compare these two approaches.

The first explicitly references the local-path storage class:

dynamic-storage-explicit.yaml

```
apiVersion: v1
kind: PersistentVolumeClaim
metadata:
  name: explicit-storage-claim
spec:
  accessModes:
    - ReadWriteOnce
  resources:
    requests:
      storage: 2Gi
  storageClassName: local-path
```

The second relies on K3s's default:

dynamic-storage-implicit.yaml

```
apiVersion: v1
kind: PersistentVolumeClaim
metadata:
  name: implicit-storage-claim
spec:
  accessModes:
    - ReadWriteOnce
  resources:
    requests:
      storage: 2Gi
```

Both achieve the same result in K3s because local-path is configured as the default storage class. However, in production environments with multiple storage options (cloud volumes, network storage, local SSD), explicitly specifying storageClassName prevents ambiguity. Use the implicit approach for learning; use explicit specification for production deployments.

We can inspect K3s's available storage classes:

```
sudo kubectl get storageclass
kubectl describe storageclass local-path
```

Notice the annotation storageclass.kubernetes.io/is-default-class: "true" on the local-path class. This designation tells Kubernetes: "When a PVC doesn't specify a storage class, use me."

Apply both examples and observe:

```
sudo kubectl apply -f dynamic-storage-explicit.yaml
sudo kubectl apply -f dynamic-storage-implicit.yaml
kubectl get pvc
kubectl get pv
```

Both PVCs transition from "Pending" to "Bound," demonstrating that K3s handles storage provisioning seamlessly whether we explicitly specify the storage class or rely on the default.

Manual PV Provisioning: Understanding the Legacy Approach

The modern dynamic provisioning approach we explored works for most use cases. However, understanding manual PV creation is valuable for advanced scenarios: migrating legacy systems, managing specialized storage backends, or working in environments where StorageClasses aren't available.

Manual provisioning requires two steps: first, create the PersistentVolume, then create a PVC that binds to it.

Create a persistent volume with a specific size and reclaim policy:

manual-storage.yaml

```yaml
apiVersion: v1
kind: PersistentVolume
metadata:
  name: reserved-storage
spec:
  storageClassName: " "
  capacity:
    storage: 1Gi
  accessModes:
    - ReadWriteOnce
  hostPath:
    path: /tmp/k8s-data
  persistentVolumeReclaimPolicy: Retain
```

Apply the PV:

```
sudo kubectl apply -f manual-storage.yaml
kubectl get pv
```

We should see our persistent volume listed with status "Available." The Retain reclaim policy means this volume won't be deleted even after the claim is removed—useful when data preservation is critical.

Now create a claim that binds to this specific volume:

manual-claim.yaml

```yaml
apiVersion: v1
kind: PersistentVolumeClaim
metadata:
  name: reserved-data
spec:
  storageClassName: " "
  accessModes:
    - ReadWriteOnce
  resources:
    requests:
      storage: 500Mi
```

Apply the claim:

```
sudo kubectl apply -f manual-claim.yaml
kubectl get pvc
```

We should see that the PVC is "Bound" to our persistent volume. Kubernetes matches the claim to the PV based on access mode and storage capacity. This manual approach gives us fine-grained control but requires careful planning in multi-pod scenarios.

When to use manual provisioning: legacy system migrations, custom storage backends without StorageClass support, and scenarios requiring specific reclaim policies like Retain.

When to prefer dynamic provisioning: new applications, rapid scaling requirements, cloud-native deployments, and learning and experimentation.

Exploring Temporary Storage: emptyDir and Network Mounts

Before diving into persistent storage, it's worth understanding the temporary storage options available within Kubernetes pods. For scenarios where we don't need data to survive pod restarts—such as caching, temporary computation, or logging—Kubernetes provides the emptyDir volume type. An emptyDir volume is created when a pod is assigned to a node, and it exists only as long as the pod runs on that node. The moment the pod is terminated or rescheduled to another node, the data is lost. This is ideal for multi-container pods that need to share scratch space or temporary files without external persistence.

Also, for distributed teams or scenarios where multiple pods need access to shared data that already exists on our network infrastructure, Kubernetes supports mounting network file shares directly into containers. The NFS (Network File System) volume type allows us to mount existing NFS exports into our pods, enabling read-write access to network-accessible storage without the complexity of full persistent volume provisioning. This approach proves particularly valuable in enterprise environments where centralized storage systems are already in place.

Example using emptyDir:

temp-storage-pod.yaml

```yaml
apiVersion: v1
kind: Pod
metadata:
  name: temp-storage-pod
spec:
  containers:
  - name: main-app
    image: nginx:latest
    volumeMounts:
    - name: scratch-space
      mountPath: /tmp/cache
  - name: sidecar
    image: alpine:latest
    volumeMounts:
    - name: scratch-space
      mountPath: /var/data
  volumes:
  - name: scratch-space
    emptyDir: {}
```

Then, also for accessing network file shares with NFS, we can use the following yaml:

nfs-mounted-pod.yaml

```yaml
apiVersion: v1
kind: Pod
metadata:
  name: nfs-mounted-pod
spec:
  containers:
  - name: app
    image: nginx:latest
    volumeMounts:
      - name: nfs-volume
        mountPath: /mnt/shared
  volumes:
  - name: nfs-volume
    nfs:
      server: 192.168.1.100
      path: "/exported/share"
      readOnly: false
```

Therefore, emptyDir is ideal for short-lived data, and direct NFS mounts are useful for sharing existing network files, but for real stateful workloads, we will usually expose that storage through a PersistentVolume and access it via a PVC so Kubernetes can manage it for us.

Note   Because both the PersistentVolume and the PersistentVolumeClaim use an empty storageClassName, Kubernetes does not trigger dynamic provisioning. Instead, it directly matches the claim to the existing PV based on access mode and capacity.

Persistent Volumes: Storage That Survives

Kubernetes provides Persistent Volumes (PVs) to solve this problem. A PV is storage that exists independently of any pod. Think of it like a USB drive that can be plugged into different computers over time.

Let's create a simple persistent volume using our K3s cluster:

nano my-storage.yaml

my-storage.yaml

```
apiVersion: v1
kind: PersistentVolume
metadata:
  name: my-storage
spec:
  capacity:
    storage: 1Gi
  accessModes:
    - ReadWriteOnce
  hostPath:
    path: /tmp/k8s-data
  persistentVolumeReclaimPolicy: Retain
```

Create the persistent volume (see Figure 16-1):

sudo kubectl apply -f my-storage.yaml

kubectl get pv

```
brando@ubuntu:~$ nano my-storage.yaml
brando@ubuntu:~$ kubectl apply -f my-storage.yaml
persistentvolume/my-storage created
brando@ubuntu:~$ kubectl get pv
NAME          CAPACITY   ACCESS MODES   RECLAIM POLICY   STATUS      CLAIM      STOR
AGECLASS   VOLUMEATTRIBUTESCLASS   REASON   AGE
my-storage    1Gi        RWO            Retain           Available
           <unset>                          6s
brando@ubuntu:~$ kubectl get pv
NAME          CAPACITY   ACCESS MODES   RECLAIM POLICY   STATUS      CLAIM      STORAGECLASS   VOLUMEATTRIBUTESCLASS   REASON   AGE
my-storage    1Gi        RWO            Retain           Available                            <unset>                          11s
brando@ubuntu:~$
```

Figure 16-1. *Creating a Kubernetes persistent volume*

We should see our persistent volume listed as "Available."

Claiming Storage with PVCs

To use a Persistent Volume, pods don't access it directly. Instead, they request storage through a Persistent Volume Claim (PVC). Think of a PVC as a reservation request for storage.

nano `my-claim.yaml`

my-claim.yaml

```
apiVersion: v1
kind: PersistentVolumeClaim
metadata:
  name: my-claim
spec:
  accessModes:
    - ReadWriteOnce
  resources:
    requests:
      storage: 500Mi
```

Create the claim:

sudo kubectl apply -f my-claim.yaml

kubectl get pvc

We should see that the PVC is "Bound" to our persistent volume. In this example, the cluster is using static provisioning: we created the PersistentVolume first, then a claim that matches it by access mode and capacity. In the next sections, we will see how K3s can also create these PersistentVolumes for us automatically using StorageClasses.

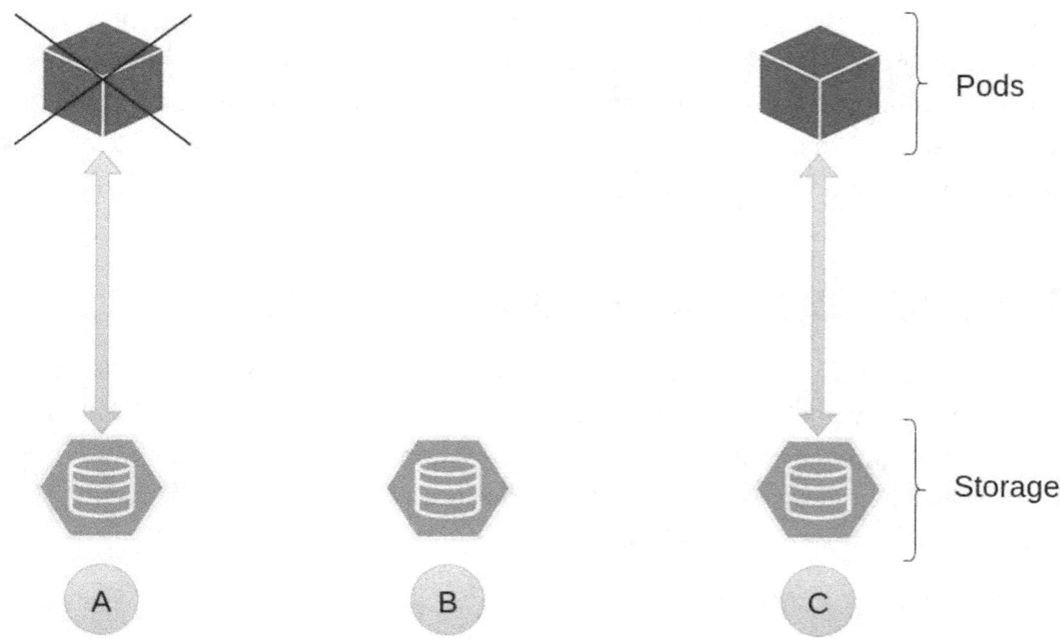

Figure 16-2. *This diagram illustrates how a pod can terminate while its persistent storage remains available and is later reused by a newly scheduled pod accessing the same data*

Figure 16-2 illustrates how Kubernetes maintains data persistence independently of pod lifecycles. The diagram demonstrates three critical phases: when pods terminate (Phase A), their associated persistent volumes remain intact, ensuring that essential application data survives independently of the ephemeral compute layer discussed in Chapter 8. During the scaling and update phase (Phase B), storage persistence enables seamless operations as pods scale, update, or recover from failures, a critical requirement for stateful applications. Phase C shows how newly scheduled pods can immediately access previously stored data through their PVCs, enabling zero-downtime deployments. In modern K3s clusters with dynamic provisioning enabled by default, this lifecycle is enhanced further: the system automatically creates the necessary PersistentVolume when we define a PersistentVolumeClaim, eliminating manual storage provisioning while maintaining the same data durability guarantees that Phases A, B, and C demonstrate.

Dynamic Storage with Storage Classes

Rather than manually creating PersistentVolumes, the modern approach in K3s is to leverage dynamic provisioning. This approach is more aligned with current Kubernetes practices and eliminates the overhead of pre-provisioning storage resources. When we create a PersistentVolumeClaim, K3s automatically creates a matching PersistentVolume based on our storage class specifications.

sudo kubectl get storageclass

Let's create a PVC that explicitly uses dynamic provisioning:

nano dynamic-claim.yaml

dynamic-claim.yaml

```
apiVersion: v1
kind: PersistentVolumeClaim
metadata:
  name: dynamic-claim
spec:
  accessModes:
    - ReadWriteOnce
  resources:
    requests:
      storage: 1Gi
  storageClassName: local-path
```

sudo kubectl apply -f dynamic-claim.yaml

kubectl get pvc

kubectl get pv

```
brando@ubuntu:~$ kubectl get storageclass
NAME                   PROVISIONER            RECLAIMPOLICY   VOLUMEBINDINGMODE      ALLOWVOLUMEEXPANSION   AGE
local-path (default)   rancher.io/local-path  Delete          WaitForFirstConsumer   false                  132d
brando@ubuntu:~$ nano dynamic-storage.yaml
brando@ubuntu:~$ kubectl apply -f dynamic-storage.yaml
persistentvolumeclaim/dynamic-claim created
brando@ubuntu:~$ kubectl get pvc
NAME            STATUS    VOLUME   CAPACITY   ACCESS MODES   STORAGECLASS   VOLU
MEATTRIBUTESCLASS    AGE
dynamic-claim   Pending                                     local-path     <uns
et>                 7s
my-claim        Pending                                     local-path     <uns
et>                 19m
brando@ubuntu:~$ kubectl get pvc
NAME            STATUS    VOLUME   CAPACITY   ACCESS MODES   STORAGECLASS   VOLUMEATTRIBUTESCLASS   AGE
dynamic-claim   Pending                                     local-path     <unset>                 17s
my-claim        Pending                                     local-path     <unset>                 19m
brando@ubuntu:~$ kubectl get pv
NAME         CAPACITY   ACCESS MODES   RECLAIM POLICY   STATUS      CLAIM   STORAGECLASS   VOLUMEATTRIBUTESCLASS   REASON   AGE
my-storage   1Gi        RWO            Retain           Available                          <unset>                         21m
brando@ubuntu:~$ nano dynamic-storage.yaml
brando@ubuntu:~$ []
```

Figure 16-3. *This shows the dynamic provisioning result where a PVC transitions from Pending to Bound, triggering automatic creation of a matching PV with local-path StorageClass*

Notice how Kubernetes automatically created a new PV for our claim! This is the power of dynamic provisioning (see Figure 16-3).

Notice the explicit storageClassName: local-path field. This directly references the default storage class. If we omit this field entirely, K3s will automatically use the default storage class, achieving the same result:

nano dynamic-storage-implicit.yaml

dynamic-storage-implicit.yaml

```
apiVersion: v1
kind: PersistentVolumeClaim
metadata:
  name: implicit-storage-claim
spec:
  accessModes:
    - ReadWriteOnce
  resources:
    requests:
      storage: 2Gi
```

Now apply both examples and observe the automatic provisioning:

sudo kubectl apply -f dynamic-storage.yaml

```
sudo kubectl apply -f dynamic-storage-implicit.yaml
```

```
kubectl get pvc
```

Watch as both PVCs transition from "Pending" to "Bound." At the same time, check the persistent volumes:

```
kubectl get pv
```

See how both PVCs are now bound to their automatically created storage? This demonstrates the efficiency of dynamic provisioning—no manual volume creation required. The local-path provisioner handles everything automatically based on the StorageClass definition. Both PVCs are now bound to their respective dynamically provisioned PersistentVolumes, demonstrating that K3s handles storage provisioning seamlessly whether we explicitly specify the storage class or rely on the default.

Cleaning Up

When we're done experimenting, clean up the resources:

```
kubectl delete pvc storage-claim
```

```
kubectl delete pvc dynamic-claim
```

```
kubectl delete pvc dynamic-claim-implicit
```

```
kubectl delete pv my-storage
```

When we delete a PersistentVolumeClaim that uses dynamic provisioning, Kubernetes automatically deletes the associated PersistentVolume as well. This happens because the local-path StorageClass has the default ReclaimPolicy set to "Delete." However, always delete PVCs before deleting PVs to ensure the reclaim policy is honored properly. If we accidentally delete a PV before its PVC, the underlying storage might not be cleaned up correctly.

Kubernetes storage might seem complex, but remember these simple concepts:

- Ephemeral volumes such as emptyDir provide storage that lasts only as long as the pod.

- Persistent Volumes provide permanent storage that survives pod restarts.

- PVCs are how pods request persistent storage.

- Storage Classes enable automatic provisioning of storage; K3s comes with the local-path provisioner enabled by default.

Understanding these basics prepares us for running real applications that need to store data permanently, like databases and file-sharing applications. As we continue our Kubernetes journey, these storage concepts will become essential tools in our toolkit.

Summary

In this chapter, we introduced the building blocks that allow Kubernetes to handle stateful workloads reliably. We contrasted ephemeral volumes like emptyDir, which disappear with the pod, with PersistentVolumes that remain available across pod lifecycles. We then saw how pods never talk to PersistentVolumes directly; instead, they request storage through PersistentVolumeClaims, and Kubernetes performs the binding based on capacity and access requirements. We explored both static and dynamic provisioning. With static provisioning, we manually created PersistentVolumes and then attached them to claims, a pattern that remains useful for legacy environments and specialized storage backends. With dynamic provisioning, we let K3s and its local-path StorageClass automatically create and manage volumes whenever a PVC is defined, which matches how modern clusters operate at scale. We also touched on integrating existing network storage via NFS, discussed reclaim policies, and cleaned up our test resources safely.

Together, these concepts give us a solid foundation for running applications that depend on durable data, from small test databases to production-grade stateful services. In the next chapter, we will shift from data persistence to workload patterns and explore how DaemonSets and Jobs help us run per-node services and run-to-completion tasks across our cluster.

CHAPTER 17

Job Management with DaemonSets and Jobs

Introduction

In the previous chapters, we've explored how Deployments and ReplicaSets manage the lifecycle of containerized applications, keeping services running continuously and scaling them across our cluster. However, not all workloads follow this pattern. Some services must run on every single node simultaneously, while others perform specific tasks that need to complete and then stop, rather than run indefinitely. Understanding these different controller types is essential for building complete Kubernetes solutions.

In this chapter, we'll investigate DaemonSets and Jobs, two critical controllers that handle workloads that Deployments cannot. DaemonSets ensure critical services like monitoring and logging run on every node in our cluster, while Jobs execute discrete tasks from start to finish. By the end of this chapter, we'll know when to use each controller and how they fit into our overall cluster architecture.

Objectives

By the end of this chapter, we will be able to

- Define DaemonSets and explain when to use them in production environments

- Create and manage DaemonSets to run services on every cluster node

© Brando Marzio Sabatini 2026

B. M. Sabatini, *Kubernetes for Absolute Beginners,* https://doi.org/10.1007/979-8-8688-2445-6_17

- Understand Jobs and distinguish them from continuously running Deployments

- Configure Jobs with completion and parallelism settings for batch workloads

- Use CronJobs to schedule Jobs automatically on a defined schedule

- Choose the appropriate controller type for different workload patterns

Building on what we learned about Deployments and ReplicaSets in Chapter 8, we now need to explore two other important Kubernetes controllers that handle different types of workloads. While Deployments are perfect for running web applications that need to stay up all the time, sometimes we need pods that work differently. Some services need to run on every single node in our cluster, and some tasks just need to finish their work and then stop. This is where DaemonSets and Jobs come in handy.

Think of it this way: if Deployments are like restaurant servers who work all day serving customers, then DaemonSets are like security guards who need to be stationed at every entrance, and Jobs are like cleaning crews who come in, do their work, and then leave when they're done.

Understanding DaemonSets

DaemonSets solve a simple problem: what if we need exactly one pod running on every node in our cluster? This happens more often than we might think. For example, if we want to collect logs from every machine or monitor the health of every node, we need one monitoring pod per node.

The beauty of DaemonSets is that they automatically handle this for us. When we add a new node to our cluster, the DaemonSet immediately creates a pod on that new node. When we remove a node, the DaemonSet cleans up the pod that was running there. We don't have to do any math or worry about keeping track of how many nodes we have.

Let's create a simple DaemonSet to see how this works. We'll make one that could collect logs from each node:

`nano log-collector-daemonset.yaml`

`log-collector-daemonset.yaml`

```yaml
apiVersion: apps/v1
kind: DaemonSet
metadata:
  name: log-collector
  labels:
    app: log-collector
spec:
  selector:
    matchLabels:
      name: log-collector
  template:
    metadata:
      labels:
        name: log-collector
    spec:
      containers:
        - name: log-collector
          image: busybox:latest
          command: ["sh", "-c", "while true; do echo 'Collecting logs...'; sleep 30; done"]
```

Notice something different from our Deployment examples? There's no replicas field! That's because DaemonSets automatically figure out how many pods they need based on how many nodes we have.

Let's create this DaemonSet:

```
sudo kubectl apply -f log-collector-daemonset.yaml
```

Now check what happened:

```
sudo kubectl get pods -o wide
```

We'll see that there's one log collector pod running on each node in our cluster. The -o wide flag shows us which node each pod is running on.

Common Uses for DaemonSets

DaemonSets are perfect for services that need to run on every node. Here are the most common examples:

Monitoring agents need to run on every node to collect information about CPU, memory, and disk usage from that specific machine. A single monitoring pod couldn't reach into every node to get this information.

Log collection services need to read log files that are stored locally on each node. Just like monitoring, we need one log collector per node to access the local files.

Network services sometimes need to run on every node to handle network traffic properly. The kube-proxy service we talked about in earlier chapters actually runs as a DaemonSet in many Kubernetes installations.

Understanding Jobs

Jobs are completely different from everything we've seen so far. While Deployments and DaemonSets focus on keeping pods running continuously, Jobs are designed to run a task until it completes successfully and then stop.

Think of Jobs like running a backup script. We want the script to start, do its work, finish successfully, and then not restart unless we specifically run it again. This is very different from a web server that should restart immediately if it crashes.

Let's create a simple Job that demonstrates this concept:

nano simple-job.yaml

simple-job.yaml

```
apiVersion: batch/v1
kind: Job
metadata:
  name: simple-backup
spec:
  template:
    spec:
      containers:
        - name: backup-container
          image: busybox:latest
          command: ["sh", "-c", "echo 'Starting backup...'; sleep 10; echo 'Backup completed!'"]
      restartPolicy: Never
```

The restartPolicy: Never is important. It tells Kubernetes not to restart the container when it finishes successfully. For Jobs, we typically use either Never or OnFailure.

Let's run this Job:

sudo kubectl apply -f simple-job.yaml

Watch what happens (see Figure 17-1):

kubectl get jobs
kubectl get pods

```
brando@ubuntu:~$ kubectl apply -f simple-job.yaml
job.batch/simple-backup created
brando@ubuntu:~$ kubectl get jobs
NAME            STATUS    COMPLETIONS   DURATION   AGE
simple-backup   Running   0/1           7s         7s
brando@ubuntu:~$ kubectl get pods
NAME                                  READY   STATUS    RESTARTS        AGE
first-pod                             1/1     Running   11 (20m ago)    34d
hello-world-5b945cc466-q66rf          1/1     Running   15 (20m ago)    139d
log-collector-m5dn8                   1/1     Running   0               6m43s
monitored-web-pod                     1/1     Running   5 (20m ago)     6d8h
my-app                                1/1     Running   90 (3m31s ago)  7d23h
simple-backup-bgfnf                   1/1     Running   0               14s
storage-test                          1/1     Running   13 (20m ago)    8d
web-app-7d7c99987c-6qpwf              1/1     Running   1 (20m ago)     3d3h
web-app-7d7c99987c-spmrm              1/1     Running   1 (20m ago)     3d3h
web-deployment-5f9bb7d6b5-42n45       1/1     Running   11 (20m ago)    34d
web-deployment-5f9bb7d6b5-ft77j       1/1     Running   11 (20m ago)    34d
web-deployment-5f9bb7d6b5-v58bh       1/1     Running   11 (20m ago)    34d
web-server-pod                        1/1     Running   4 (20m ago)     6d8h
brando@ubuntu:~$
```

Figure 17-1. *Output of kubectl apply and kubectl get jobs showing the simple-backup job running*

We'll see the Job starts a pod, the pod runs for about 10 seconds, then completes. The pod will show a status of Completed instead of Running. The Job itself will show COMPLETIONS as 1/1, meaning one pod completed successfully out of one required completion.

Working with Job Completion

Sometimes we need multiple pods to complete the same type of work. For example, maybe we have a big data processing task that can be split up. Jobs can handle this too:

nano parallel-processing.yaml

parallel-processing.yaml

```yaml
apiVersion: batch/v1
kind: Job
metadata:
  name: parallel-processing
spec:
  completions: 5
  parallelism: 2
  template:
    spec:
      containers:
        - name: processor
          image: busybox:latest
          command: ["sh", "-c", "echo 'Processing data...'; sleep 5; echo 'Done!'"]
      restartPolicy: OnFailure
```

sudo kubectl apply -f parallel-processing.yaml

This Job will run 5 pods total (completions: 5) but only 2 at a time (parallelism: 2). As each pod completes, a new one starts until all 5 have finished successfully.

Scheduled Jobs with CronJobs

Sometimes we want to run Jobs on a schedule, like backups that run every night at 2 AM. This is where CronJobs come in. CronJobs create Jobs automatically based on a time schedule.

nano nightly-backup.yaml

nightly-backup.yaml

```yaml
apiVersion: batch/v1
kind: CronJob
metadata:
  name: nightly-backup
spec:
  schedule: "0 2 * * *"
  jobTemplate:
    spec:
      template:
        spec:
          containers:
            - name: backup
              image: busybox:latest
              command: ["sh", "-c", "echo 'Running nightly backup...'; sleep 5; echo 'Backup complete!'"]
          restartPolicy: OnFailure
```

sudo kubectl apply -f nightly-backup.yaml

The schedule: "0 2 * * *" uses the same format as Linux cron jobs. It means "run at 2:00 AM every day." The five fields are: minute, hour, day of month, month, and day of week.

Choosing the Right Tool

Now that we've learned about DaemonSets and Jobs, how do we know when to use each one?

Use Deployments (from Chapter 8) when we have services that should run all the time, like web applications, APIs, or background services. These services should restart if they crash, and we might want to run multiple copies.

Use DaemonSets when we need exactly one pod per node. This is common for monitoring, logging, or network services that need to run on every machine in our cluster.

Use Jobs when we have work that needs to finish and then stop. This includes data processing, backups, database migrations, or any task that has a clear beginning and end.

Use CronJobs when we need to run Jobs on a schedule. Think daily backups, weekly reports, or monthly cleanup tasks.

Managing Job Cleanup

One thing to remember about Jobs is that they don't automatically clean themselves up. After a Job completes, both the Job and its completed pods stick around so we can check their logs or status. In a production environment, we'll want to clean these up periodically:

```
sudo kubectl delete job simple-backup
```

For CronJobs that run frequently, we can configure automatic cleanup:

```
spec:
  successfulJobsHistoryLimit: 3
  failedJobsHistoryLimit: 1
```

This keeps the three most recent successful Jobs and one failed Job for troubleshooting, automatically deleting older ones.

Putting It All Together

In a typical Kubernetes cluster, we'll often use all of these controllers together. We might have

- Deployments running our web applications and APIs

- DaemonSets collecting logs and monitoring data from every node

- Jobs processing uploaded data or generating reports

- CronJobs running regular maintenance tasks

Each controller type solves different problems, and understanding when to use each one will help us build more reliable and efficient applications. The key is matching the controller to the behavior we want: continuous operation (Deployments), one-per-node (DaemonSets), or run-to-completion (Jobs and CronJobs).

Summary

In this chapter, we examined how DaemonSets and Jobs extend our Kubernetes toolkit beyond continuously running Deployments. We explored DaemonSets as the solution for running a single pod instance on every cluster node, demonstrating their automatic synchronization as nodes are added or removed. We then shifted focus to Jobs, which execute discrete tasks with clear completion criteria, distinguishing their run-to-completion model from the long-running nature of Deployments. We covered parallel job execution for distributing work across multiple pods and introduced CronJobs as the mechanism for scheduling Jobs on predictable time intervals. Finally, we established decision criteria: use Deployments for continuous services, DaemonSets for per-node requirements, Jobs for bounded tasks, and CronJobs for scheduled execution.

In the next chapter, we'll explore DNS services in Kubernetes, understanding how service discovery and name resolution enable reliable communication between applications in our cluster.

CHAPTER 18

DNS Services in Kubernetes

Introduction

In the previous chapters, we've configured services and connected applications across our cluster, relying on stable endpoints to reach our deployments. However, IP addresses change when pods restart and services get recreated. This is where DNS becomes crucial; it provides a reliable way for applications to discover and communicate with each other by name rather than memorizing constantly changing IP addresses. This chapter explores Kubernetes' internal DNS system, CoreDNS, which automatically maintains name resolution for all services and pods in our cluster.

By the end of this chapter, we'll understand how DNS services work transparently in Kubernetes, how to query DNS names from pods, troubleshoot connectivity issues, and configure DNS for production reliability.

Objectives

By the end of this chapter, we will be able to

- Explain how DNS provides service discovery within Kubernetes clusters

- Understand DNS naming conventions and patterns in Kubernetes

- Recognize CoreDNS as our cluster's internal name server

- Perform DNS queries to test name resolution between pods and services

© Brando Marzio Sabatini 2026
B. M. Sabatini, *Kubernetes for Absolute Beginners*, https://doi.org/10.1007/979-8-8688-2445-6_18

- Troubleshoot DNS-related connectivity problems in our cluster

- Configure DNS for high availability in production environments

Building upon our network connectivity discussions from Chapter 5, where we explored how CoreDNS provides automatic name resolution for services and pods, DNS services form the backbone of communication within Kubernetes clusters. As we saw in previous chapters when working with services and deployments, being able to reach applications by name rather than constantly changing IP addresses makes cluster management much more practical and reliable.

How DNS Works in Our Kubernetes Cluster

Think of DNS in Kubernetes like a phone book for our applications. Instead of remembering complex IP addresses that change when pods restart, we can simply use names like "my-web-service" to connect to our applications. This naming system becomes essential when managing multiple services across different namespaces, as we discussed in previous chapters about organizing cluster resources.

When we created services in Chapter 5 using YAML files, Kubernetes automatically created DNS entries for those services. Every service gets a predictable name following a specific pattern that makes it easy to connect applications together. This automation removes the complexity of manually tracking IP addresses as pods come and go.

The DNS system in Kubernetes operates differently from traditional DNS servers. Rather than just resolving external domain names, it maintains a dynamic database of all services and pods within our cluster, updating automatically as resources are created, modified, or deleted.

Understanding DNS Names in Kubernetes

In previous chapters, we worked with services in the default namespace. When we create a service named *"web-service"* in the default namespace, Kubernetes generates several DNS names for it. The shortest name is simply *"web-service"*, which works from pods in the same namespace. For accessing services across namespaces, we need longer names that include the namespace information.

The complete DNS naming follows a pattern: service-name.namespace-name. svc.cluster.local. Each part serves a purpose—the service name identifies our specific service, the namespace prevents naming conflicts, *"svc"* indicates this is a service record, and *"cluster.local"* represents our cluster's domain.

This naming system integrates with the namespace concept we explored in previous chapters. Just as namespaces help organize our cluster resources, they also create DNS boundaries that prevent naming conflicts while still allowing cross-namespace communication when needed.

Figure 18-1 shows how DNS resolution operates within a Kubernetes cluster, with pods communicating directly with CoreDNS instances that run in the kube-system namespace. When pods need to resolve service names, they send DNS queries to CoreDNS, which acts as the cluster's internal DNS server and forwards external queries to upstream API servers when needed. The service naming format at the bottom follows Kubernetes' standard convention of service-name.namespace.svc.cluster.local, which enables predictable name resolution across different namespaces. This architecture ensures applications can communicate using friendly names rather than changing IP addresses, making service discovery automatic and reliable.

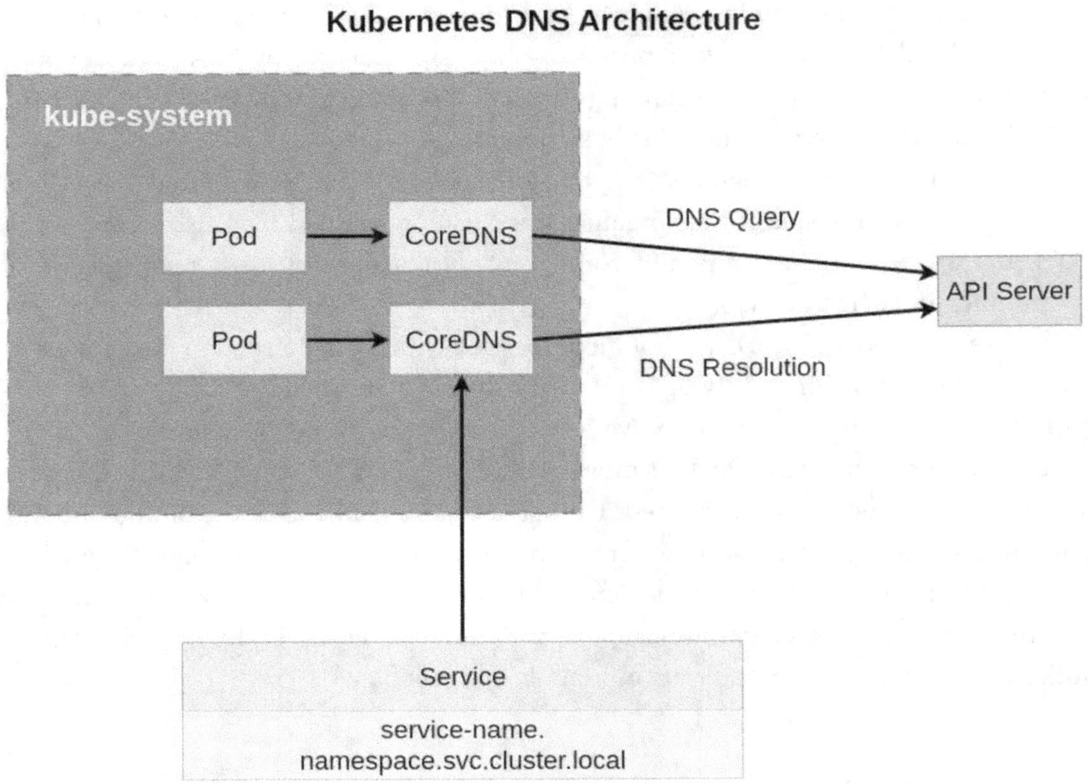

Figure 18-1. *The Kubernetes DNS architecture, showing CoreDNS resolving pod queries*

CoreDNS: Our Cluster's Name Server

From our K3s installation in Chapter 3, we already have CoreDNS running without realizing it. Unlike the traditional DNS servers we might know, CoreDNS runs as pods inside our Kubernetes cluster and stays synchronized with the API server to maintain current information about all our services.

The architecture follows the same patterns we've seen throughout this book. CoreDNS pods run in the kube-system namespace, managed by the control plane components we studied in previous chapters. The kubelet on each node automatically configures every pod to use CoreDNS for name resolution, creating a seamless experience where applications can find each other by name.

CoreDNS uses a plugin-based design that makes it incredibly flexible. The default configuration includes plugins for error logging, health monitoring, and most importantly, the Kubernetes integration that keeps DNS records synchronized with our cluster state.

Hands-On DNS Exploration with K3s

Let's explore DNS services practically using our K3s cluster from Chapter 3. This exercise will show us exactly how DNS resolution works and give us troubleshooting skills for production environments.

Verify CoreDNS Is Running

(For the scope of this specific exercise, we will run the commands as root; feel free to do so with sudo or as root.)

First, let's check that CoreDNS is operating in our cluster:

```
sudo kubectl get pods -n kube-system -l k8s-app=kube-dns
```

We should see CoreDNS pods running. K3s typically shows these as pods with names starting with "coredns".

Create a Test Pod for DNS Exploration

We need a pod with network tools to test DNS resolution. Let's create one:

```
nano dns-test-pod.yaml
```

```
dns-test-pod.yaml
```

```
apiVersion: v1
kind: Pod
metadata:
  name: dns-test
spec:
  containers:
    - name: dns-test
      image: busybox:1.28
      command: ["sh"]
      stdin: true
      tty: true
      resources:
        requests:
          cpu: "100m"
          memory: "128Mi"
        limits:
          cpu: "200m"
          memory: "256Mi"
  restartPolicy: Never
```

```
sudo kubectl apply -f dns-test-pod.yaml
```

This creates an interactive pod with network utilities. If the pod doesn't start immediately, wait a moment and try (see Figure 18-2):

```
sudo kubectl exec -it dns-test -c dns-test -- sh
```

```
root@ubuntu:/home/brando# sudo kubectl get pods
NAME                              READY   STATUS    RESTARTS         AGE
dns-test                          1/1     Running   0                67s
first-pod                         1/1     Running   4 (6h55m ago)    24d
hello-world-5b945cc466-q66rf      1/1     Running   8 (6h55m ago)    129d
web-deployment-5f9bb7d6b5-42n45   1/1     Running   4 (6h55m ago)    24d
web-deployment-5f9bb7d6b5-ft77j   1/1     Running   4 (6h55m ago)    24d
web-deployment-5f9bb7d6b5-v58bh   1/1     Running   4 (6h55m ago)    24d
```

Figure 18-2. *kubectl get pods output showing hello-world and web-deployment pods running*

Examine DNS Configuration Inside a Pod

From inside our test pod, let's look at how DNS is configured:

cat /etc/resolv.conf

We'll see output showing the nameserver IP (pointing to CoreDNS) and search domains that allow short name resolution.

Test Basic DNS Resolution

Let's test if DNS works by resolving the Kubernetes API service (see Figure 18-3):

nslookup kubernetes.default.svc.cluster.local

```
/ # cat /etc/resolv.conf
search default.svc.cluster.local svc.cluster.local cluster.local localdomain
nameserver 10.43.0.10
options ndots:5
/ # ls
bin    dev    etc    home   proc   root   sys    tmp    usr    var
/ # cd /etc/
/etc # ls
group          hosts          network        resolv.conf
hostname       localtime      passwd         shadow
/etc # cat resolv.conf
search default.svc.cluster.local svc.cluster.local cluster.local localdomain
nameserver 10.43.0.10
options ndots:5
/etc # nslookup kubernetes.default.svc.cluster.local
Server:    10.43.0.10
Address 1: 10.43.0.10 kube-dns.kube-system.svc.cluster.local

Name:      kubernetes.default.svc.cluster.local
Address 1: 10.43.0.1 kubernetes.default.svc.cluster.local
/etc # 
```

Figure 18-3. *Output of /etc/resolv.conf and nslookup showing Kubernetes DNS server 10.43.0.10*

This should successfully return an IP address, demonstrating that internal DNS resolution is functioning.

Create Services for Testing Cross-Namespace Resolution

Exit the test pod (type "exit") and create some services to experiment with:

```
sudo kubectl create deployment test-app --image=nginx:latest
sudo kubectl expose deployment test-app --port=80
```

Now create a service in a different namespace:

```
sudo kubectl create namespace production
sudo kubectl create deployment prod-app --image=nginx:latest -n production
sudo kubectl expose deployment prod-app --port=80 -n production
```

```
/etc # exit
root@ubuntu:/home/brando# sudo kubectl create deployment test-app --image=nginx:
latest
deployment.apps/test-app created
root@ubuntu:/home/brando# sudo kubectl expose deployment test-app --port=80
service/test-app exposed
root@ubuntu:/home/brando# sudo kubectl create namespace production
namespace/production created
root@ubuntu:/home/brando# sudo kubectl create deployment prod-app --image=nginx:
latest -n production
deployment.apps/prod-app created
root@ubuntu:/home/brando# sudo kubectl expose deployment prod-app --port=80 -n p
roduction
service/prod-app exposed
root@ubuntu:/home/brando# []
```

Figure 18-4. *Output showing kubectl commands creating test-app and prod-app deployments*

Now, using our existing test pod (since creating new pods requires resource specifications due to quotas):

```
sudo kubectl exec -it dns-test -c dns-test -- sh
```

Inside the pod, test these different name resolution methods:
Same namespace (short name):

```
nslookup test-app
```

Cross-namespace (namespace-qualified):

```
nslookup prod-app.production
```

Fully qualified domain name:

nslookup prod-app.production.svc.cluster.local

Exit the test pod (see Figure 18-5):

exit

```
root@ubuntu:/home/brando# sudo kubectl exec -it dns-test -c dns-test -- sh
/ # nslookup test-app
Server:    10.43.0.10
Address 1: 10.43.0.10 kube-dns.kube-system.svc.cluster.local

Name:      test-app
Address 1: 10.43.103.20 test-app.default.svc.cluster.local
/ # nslookup prod-app.production
Server:    10.43.0.10
Address 1: 10.43.0.10 kube-dns.kube-system.svc.cluster.local

Name:      prod-app.production
Address 1: 10.43.221.1 prod-app.production.svc.cluster.local
/ # nslookup prod-app.production.svc.cluster.local
Server:    10.43.0.10
Address 1: 10.43.0.10 kube-dns.kube-system.svc.cluster.local

Name:      prod-app.production.svc.cluster.local
Address 1: 10.43.221.1 prod-app.production.svc.cluster.local
/ # exit
root@ubuntu:/home/brando# 
```

Figure 18-5. *Output showing nslookup in the dns-test pod resolving test-app and prod-app services*

Now, we proceed to clean up resources.

Remove All the Test Resources We Created

sudo kubectl delete deployment test-app
sudo kubectl delete service test-app
sudo kubectl delete deployment prod-app -n production
sudo kubectl delete service prod-app -n production
sudo kubectl delete namespace production

sudo kubectl delete -f dns-test-pod.yaml

```
root@ubuntu:/home/brando# sudo kubectl delete deployment test-app
deployment.apps "test-app" deleted
root@ubuntu:/home/brando# sudo kubectl delete service test-app
service "test-app" deleted
root@ubuntu:/home/brando# sudo kubectl delete deployment prod-app -n production
deployment.apps "prod-app" deleted
root@ubuntu:/home/brando# sudo kubectl delete service prod-app -n production
service "prod-app" deleted
root@ubuntu:/home/brando# sudo kubectl delete namespace production
namespace "production" deleted
root@ubuntu:/home/brando# sudo kubectl delete -f dns-test-pod.yaml
pod "dns-test" deleted
root@ubuntu:/home/brando# []
```

Figure 18-6. *Output showing kubectl commands deleting the test-app, prod-app, and dns-test pods*

We have now completed this hands-on exercise. We've successfully explored how DNS resolution works in Kubernetes using three different methods and cleaned up all resources.

Troubleshooting DNS Problems

When applications can't find each other by name, systematic DNS troubleshooting becomes essential. The most common issues involve CoreDNS pod problems, configuration errors, or network policies blocking DNS traffic.

Start troubleshooting by checking CoreDNS pod health using the commands we just practiced. If pods are running but DNS resolution fails, examine the logs for error messages that point to specific problems.

Performance issues often appear as slow application startup or intermittent connection failures. These typically result from insufficient CoreDNS resources or too few replicas handling DNS queries for large clusters.

Network policies can also block DNS resolution by preventing pod communication with CoreDNS on UDP port 53. If applications work sporadically, investigate whether network policies are interfering with DNS traffic.

DNS Configuration for Production

Production Kubernetes clusters require careful DNS planning beyond the defaults. Running multiple CoreDNS replicas ensures high availability, while proper resource limits prevent DNS bottlenecks from affecting cluster performance.

Security considerations include monitoring DNS queries for unusual patterns, implementing proper RBAC controls for CoreDNS configuration changes, and ensuring external DNS queries use secure upstream servers.

For large clusters, advanced optimizations like NodeLocal DNSCache can dramatically improve DNS performance by running caching agents on each node. This reduces latency and network traffic by serving frequent queries locally rather than forwarding everything to the central CoreDNS instances.

Understanding DNS in Context

DNS services integrate with every other Kubernetes concept we've covered in this book. Services depend on DNS for discovery, deployments rely on DNS for multi-replica communication, and namespaces use DNS to create organizational boundaries while maintaining connectivity.

The hands-on experience with K3s demonstrates that DNS works transparently in most cases, but understanding its operation becomes crucial when troubleshooting application connectivity issues. Whether we're deploying simple web applications or complex microservices architectures, reliable DNS resolution forms the foundation that makes everything else possible.

As our Kubernetes knowledge grows beyond this beginner's guide, we'll find DNS configuration and optimization becoming increasingly important for cluster performance and reliability. The troubleshooting skills and conceptual understanding from this chapter provide the foundation for managing DNS services in production environments.

Summary

In this chapter, we explored DNS as the foundation of service discovery in Kubernetes. We examined how DNS names follow a predictable pattern, service-name.namespace. svc.cluster.local, enabling reliable application communication without hardcoding IP addresses. We investigated CoreDNS, our cluster's internal DNS server, which runs as pods in the kube-system namespace and maintains synchronization with our cluster's current state. Through hands-on exercises, we tested DNS resolution from within pods using nslookup, demonstrating same-namespace short names, cross-namespace qualified names, and fully qualified domain names. We also addressed common troubleshooting scenarios and production considerations, including CoreDNS high availability, resource allocation, and advanced optimizations like NodeLocal DNSCache.

In the next chapter, we will explore resource management, learning how to define resource requests and limits to ensure fair resource distribution across all workloads in our cluster.

CHAPTER 19

Resource Management

Introduction

Throughout our Kubernetes exploration, we've focused on deploying and managing applications across our cluster. However, managing multiple applications introduces a critical challenge: ensuring each application receives the resources it needs while preventing any single application from monopolizing the cluster's CPU and memory. This chapter addresses resource management—a fundamental aspect of running Kubernetes in shared, multi-tenant environments.

Just as infrastructure requires careful power distribution to prevent overload, Kubernetes requires intentional resource allocation to maintain stability and performance. By the end of this chapter, we'll understand how to define resource requests and limits, manage quotas at the namespace level, and ensure fair resource distribution across all workloads.

Objectives

By the end of this chapter, we will be able to

- Define resource requests and limits for containers in our YAML manifests

- Understand the distinction between CPU millicores and memory units in Kubernetes

- Create and apply ResourceQuota objects to constrain namespace resource usage

B. M. Sabatini, *Kubernetes for Absolute Beginners*, https://doi.org/10.1007/979-8-8688-2445-6_19

- Implement LimitRange policies to enforce per-container resource boundaries

- Monitor actual resource consumption using the kubectl top commands

- Configure resource management to prevent resource starvation and cluster performance degradation

When we started our Kubernetes journey, we learned how to create basic pods and saw how K3s manages our simple applications. As we progressed through the previous chapters with Deployments and ReplicaSets, we discovered how to run multiple copies of our applications reliably. Now it's time to understand how to make sure our applications get the resources they need without taking too much from other applications running in our cluster.

Think of resource management like managing electricity in our house. We have a limited amount of power coming from the electrical grid, and we need to make sure each room gets enough electricity for its lights and appliances, but we also don't want one room to use so much power that it causes problems for the rest of the house. Kubernetes resource management works the same way with computer resources like CPU and memory.

Understanding Resources in Kubernetes

Every container running in our pods needs two main types of computer resources: CPU (the brainpower) and memory (the temporary storage space). Just like our nginx containers from Chapter 6 need some CPU to process web requests and some memory to store the web pages, every application has resource needs.

In Kubernetes, we can tell our containers how much CPU and memory they need in two ways. We can set requests, which tell Kubernetes, "my container needs at least this much to work properly," and we can set limits, which tell Kubernetes, "my container should never use more than this amount." It's like telling someone, "I need at least two slices of pizza to not be hungry, but please don't give me more than four slices or I'll be too full."

CPU in Kubernetes is measured in something called millicores, or m. One full CPU core equals 1000 millicores. So if we write 250m, that means our container wants one-quarter of a CPU core. Memory is measured in normal computer units like megabytes (Mi) or gigabytes (Gi).

Setting Resource Limits in Our YAML Files

Remember in Chapter 6 when we created our first YAML files? We can add resource information to those same files. Let's look at how we modify our nginx deployment from that chapter to include resource management:

web-deployment.yaml

```
# Partial yaml file
# Reference from chapter 6
spec:
  replicas: 3
  selector:
    matchLabels:
      app: web
  template:
    metadata:
      labels:
        app: web
    spec:
      containers:
      - name: web-container
        image: nginx:latest
        ports:
        - containerPort: 80
        resources:
          requests:
            memory: "64Mi"
            cpu: "250m"
          limits:
            memory: "128Mi"
            cpu: "500m"
```

This tells Kubernetes that each of our three nginx containers needs at least 64 megabytes of memory and 250 millicores of CPU to run properly, but they should never use more than 128 megabytes of memory or 500 millicores of CPU. Since we have three replicas, our total deployment will use at least 192Mi of memory and 750m of CPU.

Resource Quotas: Setting Limits for Namespaces

Building on what we learned about namespaces in Chapter 12, we can set limits on how many total resources a namespace can use. This is called a ResourceQuota. It's like telling each department in a company, "we can spend up to this much money total, but not more."

Let's create a simple ResourceQuota YAML file:

`compute-quota.yaml`

```
apiVersion: v1
kind: ResourceQuota
metadata:
  name: compute-quota
  namespace: default
spec:
  hard:
    requests.cpu: "4"
    requests.memory: 8Gi
    limits.cpu: "8"
    limits.memory: 16Gi
    pods: "10"
```

This quota says that our development namespace can have a maximum of 10 pods, and all those pods together can request up to 4 CPU cores and 8 gigabytes of memory, with limits up to 8 CPU cores and 16 gigabytes of memory.

We create this quota the same way we created our deployments in earlier chapters:

```
nano compute-quota.yaml
```

Copy the YAML content above, then save and apply it:

```
sudo kubectl apply -f compute-quota.yaml
```

LimitRange: Setting Rules for Individual Containers

Sometimes we want to set rules about how big or small individual containers can be, rather than just limiting the total for a namespace. This is where LimitRange comes in. It's like having a rule that says, "no single person can eat more than three slices of pizza," instead of just limiting the total pizza for the whole group.

Here's a simple LimitRange example:

container-limit-range.yaml

```yaml
apiVersion: v1
kind: LimitRange
metadata:
  name: container-limit-range
  namespace: default
spec:
  limits:
    - type: Container
      max:
        cpu: "1"
        memory: "1Gi"
      min:
        cpu: "100m"
        memory: "32Mi"
      default:
        cpu: "500m"
        memory: "256Mi"
      defaultRequest:
        cpu: "250m"
        memory: "128Mi"
```

This LimitRange tells Kubernetes that in our development namespace, every container must use at least 100 millicores of CPU and 32 megabytes of memory but can never use more than 1 CPU core and 1 gigabyte of memory. If someone creates a container without specifying resources, it will automatically get 250m CPU and 128Mi memory as requests, with limits of 500m CPU and 256Mi memory.

Checking Our Resource Usage

Just like we learned to check our deployments with kubectl get deployments in Chapter 8, we can check our resource usage with simple commands.

To see how many resources our pods are actually using:

```
sudo kubectl top pods
```

To see our ResourceQuota status:

```
kubectl get resourcequota
```

```
kubectl describe resourcequota compute-quota
```

This will show us how much of our quota we're using, just like checking how much money we've spent from our budget.

Practical Exercise: Managing Resources

Let's practice what we learned by creating a deployment with resource limits, then checking how it affects our cluster. First, make sure we're in a namespace with a ResourceQuota (see Figure 19-1):

```
sudo kubectl create namespace resource-test
```

```
brando@ubuntu:~$ kubectl top pods
NAME                                CPU(cores)    MEMORY(bytes)
first-pod                           0m            14Mi
hello-world-5b945cc466-q66rf        1m            6Mi
web-deployment-5f9bb7d6b5-42n45     0m            15Mi
web-deployment-5f9bb7d6b5-ft77j     0m            4Mi
web-deployment-5f9bb7d6b5-v58bh     0m            4Mi
brando@ubuntu:~$ kubectl get resourcequota
NAME             AGE       REQUEST
LIMIT
compute-quota    6m40s     pods: 5/10, requests.cpu: 0/4, requests.memory: 0/8Gi
limits.cpu: 0/8, limits.memory: 0/16Gi
brando@ubuntu:~$ kubectl describe resourcequota compute-quota
Name:            compute-quota
Namespace:       default
Resource         Used  Hard
--------         ----  ----
limits.cpu       0     8
limits.memory    0     16Gi
pods             5     10
requests.cpu     0     4
requests.memory  0     8Gi
brando@ubuntu:~$ kubectl create namespace resource-test
namespace/resource-test created
```

Figure 19-1. *Output showing kubectl top pods and creating resource-test namespace*

kubectl config set-context --current --namespace=resource-test

Now, create a ResourceQuota for this namespace:

test-quota.yaml

```
apiVersion: v1
kind: ResourceQuota
metadata:
  name: test-quota
spec:
  hard:
    requests.cpu: "2"
    requests.memory: 2Gi
    limits.cpu: "4"
    limits.memory: 4Gi
    pods: "5"
```

Apply the quota, then try to create a deployment that asks for resources within these limits. We'll see how Kubernetes prevents us from creating more pods than our quota allows.

Why Resource Management Matters

Resource management becomes especially important when we have multiple applications running in our cluster, as we discussed in Chapter 12 with namespaces. Without proper resource management, one application might use all the available memory or CPU, causing other applications to fail or run slowly. It's like one person hogging all the food at a party—everyone else goes hungry.

By setting proper resource requests and limits, we ensure that our applications get what they need while being good neighbors to other applications in the cluster. The ResourceQuotas and LimitRanges we learned about help administrators make sure that different teams or projects can share a cluster fairly without interfering with each other.

Summary

In this chapter, we examined how to prevent resource contention in shared Kubernetes clusters. We explored resource requests, which communicate minimum resource requirements, and limits, which enforce maximum consumption thresholds for containers. We demonstrated how to specify CPU in millicores and memory in standard units within deployment manifests. We then shifted to namespace-level controls through ResourceQuota objects, enabling administrators to allocate fair resource budgets across teams and projects. We introduced LimitRange to set per-container boundaries and default values when resources aren't explicitly specified. Finally, we learned to monitor resource utilization with kubectl commands and emphasized why proper resource management is essential for preventing one application from degrading performance for others in the cluster.

In the next chapter, we will explore certificates and encryption, understanding how Kubernetes secures communication between cluster components and protects sensitive data at rest.

CHAPTER 20

Certificates and Encryption

Introduction

Throughout this book, we've progressively built a secure and fully functional Kubernetes cluster, from deploying applications to managing resources and configuring DNS. However, all of these operations depend on a foundation we haven't explicitly addressed: security. Kubernetes must ensure that only authorized users can access our cluster, that communication between components remains private, and that sensitive data is protected both in transit and at rest. This chapter demystifies certificates and encryption, the digital locks that protect our Kubernetes infrastructure from unauthorized access and data breaches.

We don't need to be a security expert to understand how Kubernetes keeps our cluster safe. By the end of this chapter, we'll grasp the fundamental concepts of certificates as digital identities, TLS as a secure communication protocol, and practical steps to protect our cluster and data.

Objectives

By the end of this chapter, we will be able to

- Understand the purpose and role of certificates as digital identities in Kubernetes

- Explain how TLS (Transport Layer Security) provides confidentiality, integrity, and authentication

- Recognize the different certificate types used throughout a Kubernetes cluster

- Describe how Certificate Authorities create and sign certificates automatically

- Understand certificate expiration and automatic renewal in modern Kubernetes systems

- Implement encryption at rest to protect sensitive data stored in our cluster

- Troubleshoot common certificate-related errors and know when to seek help

Think of Kubernetes security like protecting our house. Just as we need locks on our doors and windows, Kubernetes needs special "digital locks" called certificates to keep everything safe. Don't worry if this sounds complicated; we'll break it down into simple, easy-to-understand concepts.

In this chapter, we'll learn what certificates are and why they matter (think digital IDs), how Kubernetes uses certificates to stay secure, simple steps to keep our cluster safe, and what to do when things go wrong.

We don't need to be a security expert to understand this; just think of certificates as digital ID cards that prove who's who in our Kubernetes cluster.

Why Does Kubernetes Need Security?

Imagine our Kubernetes cluster is like a busy office building with many rooms (pods) and workers (containers). Without proper security, strangers could walk in and pretend to be employees, people could read confidential documents meant for others, and important files could be stolen or changed without anyone knowing.

Certificates are like employee ID badges in our office building analogy. Just as every worker needs an ID badge to prove who they are and what rooms they can access, every part of Kubernetes needs a certificate to prove its identity.

When we run a command like **kubectl get pods**, here's what happens behind the scenes. Our kubectl shows its "ID badge" (certificate) to Kubernetes. Kubernetes checks whether this person is allowed to see the pods. If the ID is valid, Kubernetes responds with the pod information. All of this communication is encrypted (scrambled), so no one else can read it.

To help us understand it better, the simplified diagram in Figure 20-1 illustrates the TLS handshake and mutual-TLS encryption flow between kubectl, the API server, and cluster components.

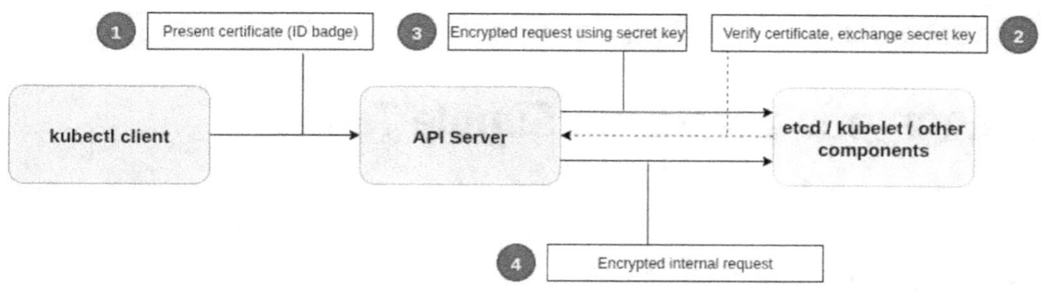

Figure 20-1. *Kubernetes API server TLS encryption and client certificate flow*

Understanding HTTPS and Secure Communication

We've probably noticed that secure websites start with "https://" instead of just "http://". The "s" stands for "secure." Kubernetes uses the same technology (called TLS) to keep all communications safe.

Think of TLS like a secret language. When two parts of Kubernetes want to talk, they first agree on a "secret code." They use this code to scramble their messages. Even if someone intercepts the message, they can't understand it without the code. Only the intended recipient can unscramble and read the message.

The simple version is this: TLS equals the technology that makes communication secure, certificates equal the digital ID that proves who we are, and encryption equals scrambling messages so only the right person can read them. That's really all you need to know as a beginner.

TLS provides three main things. Confidentiality ensures that data cannot be read by unauthorized parties through encryption. Integrity guarantees that data hasn't been modified during transmission. Authentication verifies the identity of who we're talking to through digital certificates.

How Encryption Works in Simple Terms

Kubernetes uses two main ways to scramble messages, but we don't need to worry about the technical details. Think of it like having two different types of locks.

The first type is like having the same key for our front door and back door. This is fast and works well when both people already have the same key, but the tricky part is making sure both people get the key safely.

The second type is like having a special mailbox where anyone can put mail in, but only we have the key to take mail out. This solves the key-sharing problem but is slower for big messages.

In practice, Kubernetes is smart and uses both types together. It uses the special mailbox method to safely share a regular key, then uses that regular key for the actual conversation. This gives us the security of the mailbox method with the speed of the shared key method.

Certificate Authorities in Kubernetes

At the heart of Kubernetes certificate management is something called a Certificate Authority, or CA for short. Think of the CA like the HR department in our office building analogy. Just like HR creates and distributes employee ID badges, the CA creates and signs all the certificates needed for secure communication in our cluster.

When we create a new Kubernetes cluster, it automatically sets up its own "HR department" (CA) and creates a master certificate. This master certificate then signs all other certificates in the cluster, just like how HR might use an official stamp to validate employee badges.

The master certificate lasts much longer than the individual certificates it creates, often several years. This makes sense because replacing the master certificate would be like changing the entire ID badge system in a company, which is complicated and should happen rarely.

Basic Certificate Types in Kubernetes

Don't worry about memorizing all these; just know they exist and that Kubernetes handles most of this automatically.

Server certificates are like ID badges for service desks. They prove "I am the API server" or "I am the database." When our kubectl talks to these services, it checks these certificates to make sure it's talking to the right service.

Client certificates are like employee badges that prove "I am kubectl" or "I am authorized to ask for information." Services check these certificates to identify who's making requests and whether they should respond.

The API server sits at the center of everything and needs several certificates. It needs one to prove its identity to clients like kubectl, and it needs another when it acts like a client talking to the database. Sometimes it uses the same certificate for both jobs; sometimes it uses different ones.

The database (called etcd) also needs certificates to prove who it is and to make sure only authorized components can read or write data. This prevents unauthorized access to sensitive cluster information.

Each worker node runs something called a kubelet that needs certificates for two jobs. It needs one certificate to prove its identity when talking to the main API server and another certificate because it runs its own small server that the main server uses for commands like seeing logs.

The important part is that modern Kubernetes handles most of this automatically. We usually don't need to create or manage certificates manually.

Certificate Basics for Beginners

Certificates expire, just like driver's licenses, and for the same reason. This is actually good for security because stolen certificates cannot be used forever.

The good news is that modern Kubernetes automatically renews most certificates for us. It's like having someone automatically renew your driver's license before it expires, so you never have to worry about it.

Here's what we need to know. Certificates typically last for one year by default. Kubernetes can automatically get new certificates before old ones expire. If we're using a cloud provider like Google Cloud, AWS, or Azure, they handle most of this for you automatically.

Modern Kubernetes systems increasingly rely on automatic certificate renewal. The system creates a request for a new certificate when the current one is about 30% of the way to expiring. This request gets submitted and approved automatically, and then the new certificate starts being used. For most beginners using managed services, this all happens behind the scenes without us needing to do anything.

Protecting Stored Data

While certificates handle protecting data as it travels between different parts of our cluster, Kubernetes can also protect data when it's just sitting in storage. Think of this like the difference between protecting a letter while it's being delivered versus protecting it while it's in a filing cabinet.

By default, Kubernetes stores sensitive information like passwords and API keys in a way that's not fully encrypted on disk. It's encoded, so it's not readable as plain text by humans, but it's not as secure as it could be.

Encryption at rest provides an extra layer of security. If someone managed to steal the actual storage files from our cluster, they wouldn't be able to read the sensitive information without special encryption keys. This is especially important for things like passwords, API keys, and other secret data.

To enable this protection, we configure the system with special settings that tell it which information to encrypt and how to encrypt it. Many cloud providers offer services that handle this encryption and key management automatically, so you don't have to worry about the technical details.

Configuring Encryption at Rest

To enable encryption at rest, we must configure the API server with an encryption provider configuration. This configuration specifies which resources should be encrypted and what encryption method to use. Kubernetes supports several encryption providers, including AES-GCM, AES-CBC, and secretbox.

Here's a basic example of an encryption configuration that encrypts Secret objects using AES-GCM:

key1.yaml

```yaml
apiVersion: apiserver.config.k8s.io/v1
kind: EncryptionConfiguration
resources:
  - resources:
      - secrets
    providers:
      - aescbc:
          keys:
            - name: key1
              secret: <base64-encoded-32-byte-key>
      - identity: {}
```

The configuration is passed to the API server via the **--encryption-provider-config** flag. When enabled, new Secret objects are automatically encrypted when stored in etcd, while existing secrets remain unencrypted until they are updated.

Simple Security Tips for Beginners

Starting simple is the best approach. Use a managed Kubernetes service like Google GKE, Amazon EKS, or Azure AKS because they handle security automatically. Don't worry about certificates initially; focus on learning pods, deployments, and services first. Use tools like Minikube or k3s for local learning because they set up secure clusters automatically without us needing to configure anything.

As we learn more, there are some simple guidelines to follow. Always use HTTPS when accessing our cluster, just like you would with banking websites. Don't disable security features; even if they seem complicated, they're there for good reasons. Keep your kubectl tool and cluster versions up to date because newer versions have better security.

Remember that we don't need to understand every security detail to use Kubernetes effectively. Professional Kubernetes administrators spend years learning all the security intricacies. Start with the basics and learn more advanced concepts as you become more comfortable with it.

When Things Go Wrong

Sometimes we'll see error messages that mention certificates, and they can look scary. Here are the most common ones and what they mean in simple terms.

If we see "certificate has expired," it means the certificate is too old and needs renewal, like an expired driver's license. If we see "unable to authenticate," your kubectl might not have the right permissions to do what you're asking. If you see "connection refused," you might not be connecting to the right cluster, or the cluster might be having problems.

Here are some simple things to try when we encounter problems. Try restarting kubectl or reconnecting to your cluster, as this sometimes fixes temporary issues. Check your cluster connection by running **`kubectl cluster-info`** to verify we're connected to the right cluster. Make sure your kubectl tool and cluster are recent versions because older versions sometimes have compatibility issues. Don't hesitate to ask for help by posting your error message in Kubernetes forums along with details about what you were trying to do.

What Should Beginners Do Next?

The good news is that certificate management in Kubernetes has become much more automated over time. When Kubernetes was newer, administrators had to handle many certificate tasks manually. Now, most of the complex work happens automatically.

Focus on learning in the right order. First, master the basics like pods, deployments, and services. Then learn about ConfigMaps and Secrets for storing configuration. Come back to advanced security topics like certificates when we're more comfortable with the fundamentals.

For our security learning path, start with managed Kubernetes services because they handle the complex security automatically. Practice with simple, secure setups like Minikube or k3s for local learning. Join the Kubernetes community on Slack or Reddit where we can ask questions and learn from others. Consider taking a beginner-focused security course when you feel ready for more advanced topics.

Remember that even experienced Kubernetes users don't manage certificates manually very often anymore. The tools and automation have improved dramatically. Focus on understanding the basic concepts rather than memorizing technical details. The most important thing is to build our confidence with the fundamentals first.

Summary

In this final chapter, we explored Kubernetes security through the lens of certificates and encryption. We examined how certificates function as digital ID cards that prove identity and enable secure communication between all cluster components. We learned about TLS as the technology underlying secure communication, providing confidentiality through encryption, integrity through checksums, and authentication through digital certificates. We investigated Certificate Authorities as the trusted issuers that automatically create and sign certificates for our cluster, eliminating the need for manual certificate management in modern Kubernetes. We covered certificate expiration and automatic renewal mechanisms that keep your cluster secure without requiring administrator intervention. We also addressed encryption at rest, which protects sensitive data like passwords and API keys stored in our cluster's database. Finally, we provided practical troubleshooting guidance and emphasized that automation has dramatically simplified certificate management compared to earlier Kubernetes versions.

This concludes our journey through Kubernetes for absolute beginners. From containers and pods to deployments, services, DNS, resource management, and security, we've built a comprehensive foundation in Kubernetes fundamentals. The practical knowledge you've gained positions you to continue learning advanced topics and building production-ready applications with confidence.

Congratulations on reaching the end of *Kubernetes for Absolute Beginners: Getting Familiar with K8s and Container Technologies*, covering everything from containers and pods to advanced networking, storage, and job orchestration. Thank you for choosing to read this book. I hope you enjoyed the journey and that these chapters inspire you to keep building, experimenting, and growing your Kubernetes expertise.

Index

O